TANGLED THREADS

TANGLED THREADS

Mary Barker

The Book Guild Ltd
Sussex, England

The Book Guild Ltd,
25 High Street,
Lewes, Sussex

First published 1998
© Mary Barker 1998

Set in Times
Typesetting by Innovations Marketing Limited, Bournemouth

Printed in Great Britain by
Bookcraft (Bath) Ltd, Avon

A catalogue record for this book is
available from the British Library

ISBN 1 85776 330 0

CONTENTS

ACKNOWLEDGEMENTS

I thank all the friends who have helped with this book, particularly Sheila Pharo who interviewed me for my biography; Helen Bland who typed the first draft, Jean White who read and corrected it; Margaret Tawse who has taken over and helped me find a publisher; Val Conway, Julia and Basil Everett for the photography; not forgetting East Sussex Guild of Weavers, Spinners and Dyers who have generously subscribed for colour photographs. Without all this encouragement this book would never have reached production.

INTRODUCTION

Childhood memories last a long time. In the early days of this century, someone – a nursemaid or a gardener – taught my brothers and myself a village tradition that if the numbers of the year added up to 21 that would be a lucky year. The first year this would happen would be 1929. A long, long time to wait. I seem to remember that it was that December I was offered a job in London in a contract design studio. An ambition long held, so lucky me. Not so good for the rest of the world because that was the year of the American Stock Exchange crash which ushered in ten years of dreadful unemployment that only ended with the outbreak of the Second World War. In 1938 it was Munich, and in 1947 I was demobbed from the WRNS after seven years bar six days' service to begin a new career. After that I forgot our childhood tradition.

In 1992, however, luck looked favourably on me again. Digging one day in my garden, I noticed a pain in my right leg. It did not improve so I went to my doctor. He said, 'You need a new hip,' and sent me for a free X-ray then on to a BUPA specialist. Meanwhile a letter from the Prime Minister's Office told me that I had been awarded an MBE and that I would be summoned to Buckingham Palace to receive this. It must be a dead secret until announced in the Birthday Honours in June.

The specialist told me that I must have an operation and until then walk with two sticks. I replied, 'No way.' He was annoyed, so I had to confide the reason. It was not until he was examining my legs on his couch, that he asked, making conversation, 'How did you get this decoration?'

My answer was, 'Using those two legs that you are exercising so painfully. I am a weaver!' It was, of course, politely called 'Services to Textiles'. He agreed to postpone my operation until the autumn, suggesting, not ordering, the two sticks. Due to a visit he was making to America, my operation could not be done until November.

In due course the Birthday Honours list came out and a date was set for the Investiture at Buckingham Palace. At the next meeting of the East Sussex Guild of Weavers, Spinners and Dyers, as their President, I was thanking the Guild for their present of a tape recorder to record my memoirs, when the Chairman said, 'Wait, Mary, you have more to thank us for,' and presented me with an enormous bouquet and a Super Star rose bush for my garden.

It will give me pleasure to look back to my time at Leeds University all those years ago in the 1920s. Life in the contract design studio in London was another very happy time because of all the exciting things that went on in the 1930s – the ballet, the opera, theatre, concerts, exhibitions; everything seemed new, in spite of the real recession then and the terrible unemployment.

Then came the war and my nearly seven years' service in the WRNS, which was an extraordinary thing really for an artist – to be switched from a design studio to finance and ledgers, and then paying sailors and dealing with all their problems. But curiously, I really enjoyed that. Then came demobilisation and getting back to civilian life. I did not feel I could possibly go back to the little ivory tower of a studio, having spent nearly seven years dealing with people and problems and money. My ledgers had a certain fascination! I realised I had enjoyed coping with people and problems so I put in for a WRNS officer's grant to go back to take my Art Teaching Diploma. Although I had taken some of the exams that were necessary to qualify, I had never actually gone in for teaching. For this I decided to go to Hornsey College of Art, very much recommended by a friend of mine. It took a long time for my grant to come through, and when it did they had awarded me the four years. I laughed and said, 'Straight from a grant to the old-age pension,' but of course that was really nonsense and in any case I did not retire until I was over-age.

It was a financial shock to go from the life of an officer in the services, where although your pay was not particularly good, you lived a reasonable life. My grant was £3 a week and the rent of my room was at least 30 shillings, and that meant that one had to be very, very careful. However, almost at once, the Head of Women's Crafts (which included the weaving) arranged for me to take an evening class, and the money that brought in really helped the situation.

When I qualified and got my ATD with my craft as silk weaving, I went for quite a few interviews. There was a girls' high school; and a technical school where I was to be in charge not only of the weaving but the fabric printing and pottery – to me rather a tall order – and others. I did not really want to do any of these because I had already had some teaching at Hornsey and I enjoyed teaching in an art school. Then I had an interview at Brighton Art College. They offered me one and a half days a week and I accepted that. One of them, I think it was the technical school, where I had been offered three crafts, or the girls' high school, rang up Hornsey and complained to the Principal, and the people who ran the teachers' training course, because I had turned them down. This apparently was unheard of. When taken to task, I said, 'Well, a cat may look at a king, and I really ought to be allowed to choose what will be best.' I think they were rather disconcerted by my attitude but could not do much about it. During this crisis I received yet another offer, this time to be second designer at the Royal Wilton Carpet Factory. This worried me very much indeed; I did not know whether to continue with this and tell Brighton I could not accept their one and a half days and lose my Hornsey teaching but in the end I thought, No, I have started on this freelance teaching, I enjoy it, I may have to take a day a week at some private school to make up enough money, but this is what I am going to do in the future. I am very glad I did.

The time at Brighton brought me in contact with members of the Brighton Branch of the Sussex Guild, who quickly, because several of them came to my evening class, asked me to judge their work which was going into an exhibition. Mrs Dunn was then Secretary and she came to my evening class. She said that the Committee would like it if I wrote a criticism on each piece of work that was submitted. I only had my lunch hour really free because I sometimes took a tea-hour class before catching the 9.30 train back to London. It meant I had to go to Mrs Dunn's flat, where the work was. She hastily wrote something about each piece of work. I am afraid I was pretty critical; the work did not seem to me particularly interesting and some of it definitely was not well woven, some was not well designed and quite honestly I thought the whole enterprise could do better.

Those who came to my class took their medicine manfully. I suppose they had got used to my teaching and I thought it was better to tell people pretty definitely how they could improve. I have always wanted everyone to do better work, and generally raise the standard. Probably Leeds had given me the right sort of knowledge to be helpful in most areas. Anyhow, Brighton eventually forgave me and in due course I think I replaced John Kilbride as Chairman with Dorothy Ablett as a very capable Secretary. I was still hedge-hopping between Brighton and Hornsey, which made for a tiring life, but eventually I got a full-time job in Brighton Art School – the third time of asking – and sadly left my digs in London and bought the house I live in: 1 Harrington Road down in Brighton. Of course, then there was more time to devote to the Guild and its interests. In those days we met at the Friends' Centre in Brighton. It was only a small guild. We still had an annual exhibition but everything was shown because we only had some 50 members.

When I retired I had to give up being Chairman of the Guild because I was off round the world. I had always wanted to go to sea, which I never did in my WRNs service, and through the *Quarterly Journal of the Guilds of Weavers, Spinners and Dyers* I had invitations to teach in Australia and New Zealand so I went off on a workshop lecture tour in September 1970, four days before I was officially retired, and that lasted for a whole year. Before I came home I knew that New Zealand were going to get a Queen Elizabeth II Arts Trust Grant for me to come again, so I was at home for under a year and off I went for another ten months or so.

In 1974 I went to the World Craft Council Conference in Toronto and mixed that with the same sort of lectures and workshops across North America. I visited New York, Washington, Hertford, Ottawa, Toronto and then went across country by the Canadian Railway, stopping off to teach at Edmonton and Kamloops Junction, finishing at Vancouver, where my half-sister Shirley lived. I stayed with her a month working for the Vancouver Guild, during which time I had a spell on Vancouver Island at Victoria with their guild. It was a delightfully exciting time, those four years, seeing new places, travelling around, making a great many new weaving friends.

Eventually when I settled back in England I spent more time with the Guild, which had grown tremendously in the interval and was building up to 100–150 members. We used to meet at Riverside, dear Riverside. I always loved the antique broken-down workshops and the factories and the dilapidated house on the corner. We had quite a happy spell having meetings there. During that time the Treasurer gave up suddenly and I took that over for a year, and I was then Vice Chairman and one way and another was thoroughly involved in Guild affairs. It actually was at Riverside on a snowy day in January that Margaret McLaren (a part-time weaving student from my final year at the polytechnic) was going to run me by car to the meeting and her car broke down. She had a motorbike and sidecar so she rang me up and said, 'Put on some warm clothes and I'll whiz you over in that.' It was an extraordinary journey and I put on my Peruvian poncho made of their llama wool on top of everything else (it was very warm), and I arrived windblown and was elected President. On that occasion I made it very definite that I wanted to be a working President and I have tried to be that ever since.

The Guild continued to go from strength to strength. The series of exhibitions and sales which we had first held in the Corn Exchange and later in the whole of Lewes Town Hall went well. Over the years, I used to take on the task of putting up the exhibition, which I thoroughly enjoyed. I think possibly the series of Sunday workshops that we have had for the Guild have

5

had an effect. Of course we have always had some brilliant individual members but the standard of guild members generally is rising all the time. A few years back there was a blitz on finish, which is all important. I am slightly saddened that spinners and knitters of handspun yarn outnumber the weavers. I still feel that everybody ought to have a loom but I quite appreciate the difficulties. Modern ways of living do not really allow sufficient space for looms and I think one really needs two, a small sample loom as well as a treadle loom to carry out work.

There is some splendid work being done and everybody seems to have taken to all the new methods of dyeing, dip dyeing, painted fabrics, all sorts of ingenious effects which enhance our crafts. This is the moment for me to say that we should widen our scope – I do not just mean East Sussex but the whole Association. We should shelter and encourage the other textile crafts like fabric printing and embroidery because they are all the enriching of the foundation fabric, the woven fabric, which is already there, and as we accept felting, we should exhibit these others.

The year 1992 was special for me because, as I have mentioned, I was awarded an MBE in the Birthday Honours for Services to Textile Crafts. This came as a surprise to me, but a slightly sad one; surely it was a recognition for those 32 years that I spent with the Journal? The reason I was saddened was that it came perhaps a little late in life, when so many of my friends on the Journal Committee were dead. I would have liked them to feel that they had a share in it, that they had earned it too, but that's life, isn't it? Often people do not know when they have received recognition. To me it always seems that that was the best thing that I had managed to do for textiles. I had in some ways scamped my own career so as to keep the Journal afloat, and from the moment that I became Secretary in February 1952 (I was not in on the early meetings), it somehow became my baby, and there was hardly a day when I did not have to cope with some aspect of it. It had a very hard time in its early years to survive financially. Looking back, I realise it must have been subsidised in some ways by the fact that I worked for two separate departments in two different art schools, Hornsey and

Brighton, and in both of those the Head of the Department always thought that it was something worthwhile doing and allowed me telephone calls and other help.

A few years ago East Sussex Guild gave me an exhibition, a whole stand to myself in our Annual Show at the Town Hall, to mark my 60 years as a weaver. That year, to mark my MBE, the Chairman and Committee allowed me to wear one of my caftans in the dress parade with four others worn by other people. I was very grateful for this as it ties that award to the craft of weaving. After all, it seemed appropriate to celebrate it at my Guild Show, because if it were not for all the guilds I would not have got a decoration.

Retirement gave time for me to try and fathom what gave my students and, of course, my art school friends their ideas – how the conflict between heredity and environment made them design in the way they did. My path was always very clear. All my tutors, and later the head of the studio where I worked for ten years, called me a 'natural designer'. This was not meant as a compliment. Ideas always sprang too quickly to my mind and because they came so easily they were not always developed to their full potential. Ideas should be 'tossed around', looked at from all angles and the best variations chosen. I always told my students this, but somehow could not make myself do it. In retrospect I hear my voice repeating, 'What happens if . . .' but somehow there was never enough time for me to experiment until retirement.

When given an assignment in the studio, even when announcing I could not think of anything suitable for the project, my wayward hand would be scribbling or painting roughs on any odd scrap of paper handy. From these would grow the finished design. Looking back, it is easy to see how irritating it was.

To a country child the natural world is viewed with wonder and delight. Lovingly remembered, it is a constant inspiration. Some memories are winds rippling the long meadow grasses in flowing lines, tracks made by ploughing corn, rain slowly dripping circles in pools, rain slanting silver spears against dark trees, white clouds billowing across the blue sky, climbing to make vast palaces, or chasing each other across a wind streaked sky, sea moving quietly with little frilly frothy waves edging the sand, or the angry breakers crashing noisily on the shingle. The list is endless. City shapes can bring ideas too – look at the pattern of shadows cast by buildings, the contrasting surfaces of materials, even the rainbow arabesques of petrol spilt on a wet road. Children see things clearly as shapes; later, knowledge and the desire for accuracy complicates vision. Thought distils abstract forms from the rhythm and pattern of growth and movement.

1

Early Years

My father was Director at about the age of 29 of the Fruit and Cider Research Station at Long Ashton, near Bristol, and this village was where I was born.

Soon after I was two years old I had a brother and before I was four there was another. So the boys and I grew up really rather like puppies in a basket. We were tremendous friends. We had a

Mother and Mary

cousin who was five months or so younger than myself and because he was an only child he spent most of the holidays with us, so we grew up in this happy situation. The grown-ups always said, 'Bet' – that was me – 'always plans the mischief and the boys carry it out.' We lived in a tall semi-detached Georgian house with cellars. It was built on the side of the hill so that the kitchen and scullery were on ground level at the back of the house, opening onto a terrace with a flight of steep steps down to the lawn and vegetable garden, but at the front of the house it was as though it was a basement. There were steps down from the flagged passage that led to the kitchen to a cellar dug deep in the ground of the hill. We were never, as children, allowed to go down below there, but it was very dark at the corner where the kitchen stairs led down this passage and we used to frighten my small brother by telling him that some mysterious animal called Fever-fever lived in the cellar and might come out even from underneath the cellar door. The poor boy was terrified.

The house had a stable on the side but I do not remember much about that. I do remember tall windows with narrow bars between the panes looking down the garden to the valley, the cricket pitch and then the hills slowly rising until eventually Dundry crowned the furthest hill. The little church and the village looked tremendous sitting up there tight on the crest.

Our nursery had those square windows that rooms at the top of the house had to have in Georgian façades. One of my very vivid early memories was of my brother, the one two years younger than I, being given a football when he was about three. Father attempted to show Norman how to use this. His first kick hit a picture that my mother was very fond of and she screamed out; but with his second effort (which we all considered successful) he kicked the ball right through one of the window panes. Unfortunately our nanny was for some reason scrubbing the front door steps three floors below and she thought it was my brother Norman, though how he could have done it at his tender age, I do not know. She dashed upstairs into the nursery crying: 'You naughty boy, what have you done?' Mother and Father were shrieking with laughter and we all thought it was a tremendous joke, but Nanny was really cross with Pa.

My father loved small children, even babies. He said he enjoyed watching a baby's development, how they began to notice things around them, the look of wonder when they discovered their own two hands and held them up watching their movements. As he had six children, five in his first family and later my half-sister, Shirley, he had plenty of opportunity to study them. He teased us all except Anne and had a wonderful serial story to entertain us which had a refrain, 'I will give you three guesses', when he came to difficult parts. Needless to say our guesses were always wrong but they gave him ideas and time to provide his solution. This never-ending story infuriated both Mother and Nanny.

He had one sister with a husband and son, Kenneth, who came to stay with us, plus the grandparents, each Easter. We went on holiday with them, too, and the whole family spent Christmas at Cambridge.

In those dim, distant days – I was born in 1907 – ladies stayed in bed quite a long time after their confinement. Of course, the birth was at home, with a monthly nurse coming to stay. One of my very early memories was the Christmas after my young brother Aubrey had been born on 12 December. A Christmas tree had been dragged upstairs and semi-hidden behind Mother's dressing table. Eventually the great day dawned. Even the baby was brought in and sat up on the pillows beside Mother and then the excitement began, the lovely things being cut down off the tree. I remember exactly how they looked to this very day. A little pair of chocolate scissors wrapped in gold paper was given to me. I was already fond of trying to make things.

Another memory, again of Mother's bedroom – we were in her bed and it was about getting up time in the morning. Nanny rushed upstairs, knocked at the door and came in and said: 'The King is dead' (that was Edward VII). Mother burst into tears, which seemed a bit excessive, and in the excitement Norman tumbled off the bed and walked his first steps. He must have been about 18 months.

I recall another day when my mother was leading me along the road when we met a villager with her little girl wearing a straw bonnet with tiny silk rosebuds and a pink pelisse (little

Kenneth and Mary 1908

coat) to match. I recognised my favourite outfit and threw myself down, kicking and screaming. At this moment, to Mother's embarrassment, Lady Smyth, the lady of the manor, came by in her carriage and pair. She stopped and said, 'My dear Det' – Mother's pet name – 'whatever is the matter?' Mother, laughing and blushing, tried to explain that she had given away my coat that I had grown out of. The footman got down and picked me up and we were driven home in fine style.

For my third birthday Mother had papered the inside of a large oblong packing case with wallpaper and painted the outside red. My grandparents had given me a set of white furniture and all of my dolls, clad in new mauve dresses smocked in green (suffragette colours), were sitting waiting for me, each carrying a tiny gift. In due course I saw the furniture in my niece's daughters' playroom.

Father taught me to read early, I could read the Pat-pet-pit-pot-put book by the time I was four years old and have been a bookworm ever since. One day Norman and I were on the rug in front of the fire and he was tearing the pages of my *Alice in Wonderland* book. I grabbed it from him. It was a big heavy book, so I held it clasped to me and began to cross over to Mother, but there was a fold in the hearth rug. I tripped over and cut open my forehead on the ornate fireguard – blood spurted out everywhere. Later I remember Father holding me under an oil lamp while the doctor sewed me up. I can still see that lamp with its long brass stem and ornate top that supported the round white glass lampshade. To this day the scar remains.

The boys and I played in the garden down the long, steep flight of stone stairs. Aubrey had grown out of his habit of crawling over flower beds and scooping up bugs and beetles which he attempted to eat, and had begun to try to climb the fig tree like Norman and myself. One day he fell and got caught up by a spike sticking into his corduroy pants. I watched him turning purple in the face and as we could not lift him down I sent Norman to fetch help. He plodded up the garden steps, did not tell Nanny who was in the kitchen, but plodded on up a further three flights to the top of the house to find Mother. 'Mummy, come quick, your little boy is hanging in the fig tree.' Mother flew down those stairs to find Aubrey going black in the face while I watched with interest. After that, branches were cut away and the fig tree pronounced a forbidden climb.

House on Long Ashton main road

One day Mother took Norman and me into Bristol – she said we were going to a bank. We were quite excited but when we got there it was only a funny sort of shop with men behind a counter peering out of hatches. Mother was laughing and talking to one of them but Norman got fed up and asked, 'Where is the river?' This produced more laughter and then an explanation, but we felt how stupid grown-ups were.

A regular outing with Mother was to go to the dentist. We hated this ordeal. It was a long walk from the tramway terminus and we lagged behind our determined mama. Norman kept moaning and saying he felt sick. Mother, exasperated, yelled to him, 'Be sick then,' and he was, much to my and Aubrey's delight. We were still taken to the dentist.

Mother driving family
to Mabel's wedding

Nanny (Mabel) moved to the new house with us and stayed until Peggy was two years old. She had been 'walking out' with her young man for years and years and at last decided to marry him. Mabel lived in a village about seven miles away. Of course, we all wanted to go so Mother, to our amazement, borrowed a pony and trap and drove us four, all dressed up in our best, to the wedding. When we got to the cottage Mabel dashed downstairs, gave a scream of horror, and took 'her children' upstairs to tidy us up. She washed our hands and faces, even our ears, combed my long gold hair, twiddled Peggy's curls, retied hair ribbons and then dealt with the boys. Only then did she don her wedding veil. Mother was not a bit abashed, she had enjoyed showing us that she could harness and drive a trap and feed and water the pony. She had spent a great deal of her childhood on her grandfather's farm. We were surprised at her skill.

Father believed that his children should learn the taste of alcohol early and I well remember Anne's first Christmas dinner (1921). She was propped in a laundry basket beside Father and when champagne was opened he gave us all a little in our wineglasses then filled a dessertspoon for Anne to sip. Mother screamed in protest, but Anne lapped it up.

In those days Long Ashton was a proper village. Everything centred round the church and the cricket field. Father played the organ in church. The Vicar had a lively family of young people who became great friends of Mother and Father, and Father did something for the cricket, but he was never very good at games. It was a very happy time then. Norman and I used to be put across the road on a Saturday morning, clutching a penny, which was our week's pocket money, and we toddled down on our own to the village shop. There we expended our wealth on a variety of sweets. Funnily enough, you could get quite a bit for a penny in those days.

There was a horse-drawn bus coming out to the village. People had to walk a mile and a half into what was then called 'the trams' – the tramway terminus at Ashton Gate. Father and Mother were great theatregoers and they used to walk all the way home from Bristol after the theatre at night. On bank holidays and other special times, such as works holidays, parties from the works came out in what we called brakes, which were covered waggons where you sat down the two long sides facing one another. There were straps to hang from in the middle. These brakes were covered with iron hoops and there was an awning over them. They must have got rather wet if bank holidays then were as rainy as they are now.

Looking back, I think the other house that influenced me and started my fondness for period houses was the one that belonged to my grandparents. This stood in the middle of a terrace of Georgian houses, it was the centre house, called Glen Avon, in Maids Causeway, Cambridge, looking out over the Midsummer Common to the river and the university boathouses. It had a pillared porch, quite dramatic, with long windows on either side. The basement had one front room, which was the maids' sitting room normally, and this was always given over to us children as a playroom when we stayed there at Christmas and other holiday times. The back of the house, though, was what impressed me most. There was a long terrace with steps in the centre going down to the lawn. The terrace, although it had wrought-iron railings, had been glassed in to make it warmer to sit in. The drawing room and the billiard room both opened their four long windows onto this terrace and at the far drawing room end, part had been shut in to make a conservatory where my little gran grew her precious pot plants.

GLEN AVON 5 MAIDS CAUSEWAY, CAMBRIDGE
circa 1780

I fell in love with my own house here at Brighton at first sight. It has a hooded balcony similar to the Cambridge house, with the steps leading down to the lawn onto which opens my sitting room and studio-kitchen. There was once a beautiful long room which was divided for convenience. My bedroom, which is the original dining room of the house, with a study beyond now included, has a small Regency-type bay window. Although these features are Regency, the house was built semi-detached in about 1844–45 so it is early Victorian. This was probably an advantage because in the Regency period the houses were thrown up very quickly and sometimes rather shoddily. I have had various bothers with mine, but on the whole it is well built.

A few years ago I had a serious burglary and lost several pieces of furniture that I had inherited from my grandparents' home, including two mirrors which the valuer told me to call pier glasses. He was very interested in my description of these and a drawing I had made, and asked if I could remember any other things that might have gone with the house and whether they were there when my grandparents bought the house. Naturally I did not know, but I could tell him that there were the 'naked ladies', obviously fittings, otherwise my grandmother would never, never have had them. These were two statues, a lightly draped nymph which stood at the foot of the stairs, and upstairs where there was a small flight of stairs leading up to the two best bedrooms from the landing, on I suppose a plinth or cupboard, under the window that looked down this little passage was another naked lady, kneeling. We children admired them very much. When the valuer heard these described and that they had been adapted to hold lamps in their outstretched arms he said, 'Oh, then I am pretty sure that you have been robbed of a pair of Chippendale mirrors – where did they hang?' When I told him on either side of a big marble mantelpiece in the drawing room he felt convinced. He said we could not put them in because we had no real proof, but he felt convinced that that was what they must have been. I was very grieved; I loved my mirrors and so did my nephew.

To go back to Long Ashton and our home – when I was seven I think Father found that we were going to be too many for the house, so he built a house up on the side of the hill beside the golf course. He was already very fond of golf and spent a lot of time up there. Of course this was blissful for the children. We had lovely fun with Johnny Builder and Curly Builder and the others. They would give us rides in wheelbarrows along narrow plank bridges over the dugout foundations. One day we were given lunch very early in the kitchen and then sent off with the kitchen-maid to go to the building site. We were not taken home until it was getting dark – it was February. When we got there Father was waiting for us on the doorstep with a white bundle in his arms, very excited. 'Say hello to your new sister,' he said. We had a look at a tiny red screwed-up face, not very interested. A week or two later I was sat in Mother's basket chair, landed with the job of giving the baby its bottle.

Eventually on a most fateful date in July 1914 the house was finished and we moved into it.

We were going on holiday, as usual, to Bournemouth and there was all this talk of war so I asked Father why we were going to war. What was wrong? He told me then that the Grand Duke and his bride had been assassinated in Sarajevo and tried to explain the business of treaties and how this led to all the countries being drawn into the conflict. Even now, to my generation the sound of that word 'Sarajevo' tolls a warning bell, so does 'ethnic cleansing', so reminiscent of the Nazis and their 'racial purity' to excuse their treatment of the Jews. Today, sights and sounds of war appear on television in our sitting rooms, often at supper-time. Perhaps a diet of violence on film and TV has deadened the impact of the horrors we see of people suffering. After all, one has to be over 50 years old to recall what air raids were like in the 1939–45 World War. I do remember that when we got to Bournemouth Father would dig great big round sandpits for us all to sit in out of the wind to eat our picnic lunch and wardens would come to the beach telling him to fill them in before we went home in the evening.

Children were treated quite toughly in those days. When I first had two little brothers, there was only room in the pram for Aubrey and Norman and I had, at the age of four, to walk. Now our nurse used to take us one day up the road to the Research Station, a walk of about a mile, and back, and just occasionally my little brother Norman, who was nearly square (aged about two) would be lifted out so that I could have a little ride, but on the whole I used to walk all that way. The following day Nanny would take us down to the tramcar terminus, which was another walk of a mile plus. So we grew up expecting to walk.

When we first moved into the house at Golf Lane the boys and I had a governess, the daughter of the retired schoolmaster who was one of Father's golfing partners. But in about a year when it seemed that it was going to be a long war, we were sent to school in Bristol. I went to Clifton High School, and the boys to Colchester House, which was a preparatory school for Clifton College. Aubrey was not quite five and had to go to the Clifton High School Kindergarten first, where he met his lifelong friend Ben Round, who afterwards became my brother-in-law.

In our long walk to school young brother Aubrey could be a trial. Brother Norman at six and a half and at prep school felt that life was now *real* and one should be punctual. Aubrey believed in enjoying the given moment. His pleasure was to walk along the top of a rough stone wall. This slowed progress and he fell behind us. Imagine our envy one day when he sailed past perched on the bicycle carrier of his friend 'the white lady'. We called her this because she invariably wore a white top and, when fine, a white hat. She must have worked in an office somewhere en route because she dropped Aubrey before we reached the docks. We had to run to catch him up before he attempted that fascinating but dangerous promenade over the lock gates, deep water on one side and a long drop to sludgy mud the other. A little way downstream we could look up to the Clifton Suspension Bridge spanning the gorge, with Leigh Woods on the left hand, the crescents of Clifton above and Hotwells on the right.

The swing bridge across the River Avon down at the basin had to be mended. It was mostly kept open. It may have been a precaution against having it damaged and struck by Zeppelin raids. Anyway, the only way for us to cross this river was to walk in single file along the dock bay. It was a double bay with iron posts and chains that you could hold on to between the posts, but further on there was no support. We usually walked in single file with young Aubrey in the middle. We had walked all the way from Long Ashton, which was a good three-mile walk, and then we had to go across Hotwells and up Clifton Vale, a very steep hill to Clifton, and to our respective schools.

Later other children from the village joined us, including Reggie Verdon-Smith, the future Sir Reginald and a distinguished businessman; in those days he used to pretend he was a puffer train and run diagonally up and down to make the long hill less boring.

At the end of morning school I had to go over to the kindergarten to find Aubrey and set him in the right direction to walk home, hoping that Providence would supply an escort to get him across the bridge. After lunch and prep it was my turn to walk home and I was supposed to get there before dusk. Often I caught Aubrey up on the way. Sometimes we were lucky and had a lift from the baker's cart or a passing pony and trap. One day we had an adventure. Motor cars were rare – our grandfather at Cambridge had one lined with grey cord with a cut-glass vase for flowers – so we were thrilled when a man in a two-seater picked us up. The engine was making funny noises when we reached the Angel Inn. The driver stopped, showed me a pedal he wanted me to keep my foot on and lifted Aubrey out. There was a water

21

trough where horses drank and we were startled to see the man fill his hat with water and run back to the car. Smoke was coming from the bonnet and there was red flame near my foot. I jumped out and men rushed from the inn with sacks to beat out the flames. We watched for a while, then as no one took any notice of us we walked the last quarter of a mile home.

We children were given a lot of freedom. At home, we only had to nip over a fence at the back of our garden and we could be into the meadows running up to the golf course that ran along the top of the hill. Nobody questioned that we should go and do just what we liked. As long as we turned up promptly to meals, and instinct like a young animal always took us back at the right time, no one worried very much what we did. So we were able to invent our games and have a wonderful, lively, free childhood. Imagine children being allowed to do that in this day and age.

Rationing in the war became pretty acute. I suppose we did not notice very much because we had a large garden and grew plenty of fruit and vegetables, which could be augmented by produce from the Research Station. The butter ration was only a little pat, possibly one and a half inches by an inch, and the children's individual butter rations were put on plates from my doll's tea service. Some of us saved it up to nearly the end of the week for a glorious spread, the others were very miserly and they sometimes fell foul of the kitchen, because those who had left most lost it when a cake or pudding was in view. One learned to be canny.

I remember this war as a much sadder one than the Second World War. There was never a morning, or so it seemed, when at school prayers the headmistress was not telling us that some girl had stayed away because her father, or elder brother, had been killed, and so it went on, always the younger men being killed off. (The Second World War seemed in a way fairer because the casualty lists included men, women and children killed in the bombing raids. We were all in it together.)

In the 1914–18 war I can remember Mother and my aunt Gwen, still alive in 1993 at the age of 97 or 98, dressing up in very fetching VAD uniforms and going down to Long Ashton Court to help with the wounded officers in the hospital there.

22

Their white caps had a large red cross on the front and were tied tightly round the head, springing out into starched butterfly wings at the back.

At the Court, which stood in its own park with herds of wild deer, the long south terrace had been turned into a lounge for convalescent patients. They wore bright blue uniforms and sat or lay on reclining chairs among tea tables. Some could stagger on sticks or crutches down the steps to the formal garden with green hedges and bright flower beds. My memory is always of sunny visits. When I was taken along too it was all great fun. People seemed very cheerful and they just got worried towards the time when their wounds were nearly cured.

Mother was dark-haired with lively brown eyes, very vivacious, and she thoroughly enjoyed flirting with the officers. Her sister Gwen, aged then about 20, had chestnut hair and hazel eyes and was at that time a quiet girl. Many years later, however, my brothers voted her the sexiest of Mother's four sisters; this was high praise as two, Kathleen and Margery, were lively blue-eyed blondes and their elder sister Dorothy was the beauty of the family, with very dark hair, blue eyes and a serious disposition. In their home town of Cambridge they were known as 'the beautiful Miss Normans'. They were all experts with a punt pole on the River Cam and had a wonderful time at river picnics with the undergraduates. Margery, who was ten years older than myself, has often told me how well Grandma dressed them all. She described their cream covert coats worn with panama hats, those for the elder two trimmed with roses, while the younger, Gwen and Margery, had wreaths of field flowers, daisies and buttercups. Mother, who married at 21, must have rebelled against Grandma's choice of clothes because in our dressing-up box was a pre-war (1914) gown of salmon pink, crinkly silk, covered with black spotted net and hobble skirt, with a picture black hat trimmed with two water lilies. We children treasured this for years.

2

World War I and After

The Golf Lane house had been built for entertaining. It was a generous size with seven bedrooms, drawing room, dining room, billiard room a wide hall and all the usual offices, and room to expand. In fact a far drawing room was built on to house Father's grand piano, a present from his mama, our little gran. She was tiny but had an indomitable will. She had turned Pa into a fine musician by compelling him to his daily practice as soon as he got in from school – he also studied the violin and could play the organ in church.

Father spent half of most weeks in London during the war. This was in connection with his work for the Ministry of Food. He stayed nights at the Regent Palace Hotel just off Piccadilly, and we children were thrilled to hear his description of air raids. He told us how one night he had woken to the noise of broken glass. He knocked at the next door room where a friend of his was sleeping. They had left their shoes outside the door overnight to be cleaned and these had been collected by the night porter. So down they went in their socks and padded out into the street, over broken glass, to see the damage to the Circus. Eros was still standing on his plinth.

He also belonged to some organisation called the Artist Rifles. They did sentry duty at the suspension bridge and other landmarks in Clifton and Bristol. I suppose this was a forerunner of the Home Guard in World War II. Anyway, he made friends there with the musician Hubert Parsons, who often came out to Long Ashton to play duets with him.

After our holiday in Bournemouth, we returned to the excitement of moving to our new house. Mother intended to send us all to Cambridge to be out of the way but Father was adamant. He insisted that he and Maudie had had all the fun of moving house when they were young and his children should have the same enjoyment. One of the Research Station staff wives had the baby Peggy, now six months old, for the whole day. The boys and I went down for lunch and we had a splendid time riding on the lorries, making friends with the moving men, keeping the odd builders still finishing outside drains informed about what was happening and generally getting under everyone's feet. The grown-ups must have felt very relieved when an exasperated Mabel announced, 'Enough is enough,' and marched us off to bed after a hasty but very necessary dip in the new bath. We fell asleep at once but had had a wonderful day to remember.

There was one disadvantage in living in this new house; we had to decide whether to play in the lower garden or the upper one each morning. This was because the house took up nearly the whole width of the plot Father had bought and as baby Peggy was sleeping in her pram on the veranda, we were not allowed to pass her for fear she would wake up. She was already yearning to grow up and join us in our games. This yearning was to continue for at least three more years. To this day I can visualise her small figure as she tried to run after us along the drive. 'Where are you going?' she would cry, and we would shout back, 'To the Ha Ha Tree.' This was an old yew tree on top of the drive bank and quite impossible for a three-year-old. Eventually we did allow her to join in – but then when she was seven, Anne was born; Peggy was put back to the nursery while we three had schoolroom status.

The village school was at the foot of our garden, its decorative spire soared up over the raised end of the tennis court. One of our favourite plays for down garden mornings was to stand along the fence dividing our garden from the school playground and make friends or enemies of the children. Later on Father bought the meadow and orchard adjoining and eventually added the school vegetable gardens, which stretched right down to the main road. We then acquired a gardener and a garden boy to cultivate this enlarged property. All our garden boys became dear friends and taught us how to smoke behind the gooseberry bushes. An ornamental pond was dug with a shallow rim around a deep centre. The boys and I were used to this and never fell in but later both Peggy's and Anne's friends who came to play were always having to be fished out and sent home dripping. Mother had an answer to this problem. She announced that whoever fell in the pond accidentally or on purpose was to be fined sixpence *out of their own pocket money*. This edict stopped the epidemic of half-drowned children. At one penny a week no one felt wealthy enough to risk the expense!

Once we went to school and acquired friends, our house became a boon to our friends' parents. No one ever seemed to mind how many extras there were for lunch. Ben, who was Aubrey's buddy from the age of six, was always tapping at the drawing room door and saying, 'Mrs Barker, I've lost the last bus again – will you ring Mum, and I'll just pop into Norman's bed for the night.' We rejoiced in our telephone. Our number was Long Ashton 12.

Father was super at organising parties – either tennis or Christmas ones. We usually had three. One was for those whose hospitality must be returned; this included any friends who might not fit in. Then another for the little girls, and finally the super one for our best friends with one or two grown-ups with talent to help Father get going with his beloved game of charades. The programme was always the same, a guessing game on arrival, a name being pinned on your back which you had to guess by asking questions. The answer could only be Yes or No. This broke the ice. Then perhaps musical chairs or pass the parcel – later on we took to murder and hid happily round the house. There followed supper, always a delicious spread, to be followed by charades. Two grown-ups picked sides, as tactfully as possible dividing the talent. One side retired to the drawing room and settled down as audience, the other rushed into the billiard room, decided on a word, usually with two syllables, and thought up a three-act drama – one syllable per act, with the final word in the third act. Parts were allocated, everyone dressed up and collected props and rushed on stage to play their part. The audience was happy in the intervals, led by their grown-ups, trying to guess. Sometimes people had a lucky idea and hit on the word, sometimes not. Mother took no part in these displays. She sat or lay on her couch watching. She would sometimes shriek with indignation when some valuable prop was brought on. I well remember one occasion when a real baby was needed, not a doll dressed up. Father raided the night nursery for Anne, who was about six months old. She was behaving quite amiably, acting her part well, when Mother noticed. She screamed, 'My baby, my baby,' rushed on stage and tried to remove Anne. Everyone collapsed with laughter and Anne thoroughly enjoyed her moment of fame.

When brother Aubrey died, a few years ago, I had a letter from a school friend I had not seen for years. After condoling with me, she harked back to those parties in which she and Aubrey had happily taken part some 70 years ago. The Barkers' parties were famous in Clifton during our growing-up years.

Mother and Father played bridge. It was the simpler version, auction; contract had not yet been invented. They gave bridge parties fairly often. The boys and I played our version in the billiard room, particularly when Kenneth was staying with us to make up a four. Mother tried to teach us how to play properly. One of her lessons was to make us call a no trump on any hand not a yarborough. We might never make it but we were to try for as many tricks as possible. Good training. Anne, aged four or five, knew plenty about bridge from Mother. When Mother had a ladies' bridge four, Anne would come in when tea was brought in. If they were finishing a hand, she would stand behind a player watching closely. If the poor lady did not make her call, Anne would observe, 'You should have finessed your queen,' or some equally unfortunate remark.

When I told this anecdote years later, it nearly caused a car smash. I was being given a lift home by my bridge teachers Jonathan and Jackie.

'She must be a brilliant player.' Jonathan said.

'Oh no,' I replied, 'she won't play now. She despises bridge as a waste of time.'

I always dreaded the bridge parties. If someone dropped out at the last minute, I was press-ganged to make a four. I had to rush upstairs to find a party frock, brush my hair and try not to panic. I was always allowed to start off with Father as my partner, but then one had to move after four hands. He had been known to give me a spot of brandy in the pantry to provide a little Dutch courage.

Aubrey and Ben left Clifton High School Kindergarten – a great relief to the staff – for prep school Colchester House with Norman. There had been a fancy dress party at school, possibly to celebrate some victory. Mother asked questions about it at lunchtime. Aubrey piped up that our headmistress was already wearing her fancy dress at morning prayers. Mother asked what this costume was. 'Oh,' said Aubrey, 'Queen of the Butterflies.' The head was a large lady, distinctly unglamorous, but a popular speaker at chamber dinners and public meetings. Of course, her costume was her academic cap and gown. Dear Pips used this tale in her speeches for years to come.

Colchester House believed in theatricals. Each Christmas the boys acted in a play. Both Norman and Aubrey were star performers. Peggy was taken to see the play, *The Queen of Hearts.* Ben by now was tall for his age, no actor but the centre-piece of the chorus. Aubrey was the Knave and Norman the King. Peggy was driven home in a dreamlike trance. It was her first play and she announced that she had fallen in love with Ben. When asked why, she said it was the pink light shining through his sticky-out ears. She was faithful to her first love; she married him 20 years later. Aubrey too was to marry a childhood friend, Alice Marshall, a farmer's daughter from the village. Alice and I attended the same confirmation class at the vicarage. It was good luck for myself and Norman as it kept our family circle close all the rest of our lives.

Colchester House happened to have a copy of Dr Marie Stopes's textbook floating around among the boys. My brothers thought I had better share the detailed information too so they brought it home for me to read. I suppose we learnt some technical details but country children have eyes that see what happens in the animal world. Some years after this, I was about 14 years old at the time, poor Mother was detailed off to tell us the 'facts of life'. She had a silent audience; we dared not look at one another or we would have got the giggles. She was very embarrassed. Afterwards we agreed she had tried but could not give her very good marks.

Sex education did not begin in schools until Peggy and Ben's daughter, again at Clifton High School, was about 12. Peggy said her daughter was talking about Hum. B. as a subject. She asked what this was and was told human biology. She or Ben used to sneak looks at her textbooks overnight.

By this date, I was teaching in art schools and was aware our little dears would have had sex education. My view was that it was a little dangerous – children would think, we do homework for other lessons, perhaps we had better go behind the bicycle sheds for this. The constant number of teenage pregnancies to this day gives a certain validity to my point of view.

News filtered through to the village that the Armistice was to be signed on 11 November. Father was determined to be in London for the Great Day. He and Mother scurried round the village borrowing ready cash from friends. They were off at daybreak by the early train. The boys and I went to school as usual. At 10.45 a.m. the girls were mustered in the hall. The headmistress came in and we all sat quiet, waiting. The windows and doors were left open. At long last, pandemonium broke out, church bells rang, factories sounded their hooters, ships in the docks blew their sirens; traffic stopped for a moment. The headmistress read a Collect of Thankfulness and asked us to remember that this was a sad, difficult day for those girls who had lost a father or a brother. She then announced a holiday so we hurried off home. Father and Mother arrived back the next day, exhausted by their celebrations. They had stood in the crowd outside Buckingham Palace, cheering the King, Queen and Royal Family. They had dined well, gone to the theatre and joined the midnight crowds around Lord Nelson's statue in Trafalgar Square.

Nearly 27 years later, on VJ Day, I remembered this. I was staying at the Mead on leave for two or three days; my brother Norman was there with his daughter Angela. Stepmama Alicia thought we ought to celebrate the occasion, so we all, including

29

Peggy and family, climbed into cars and went to the sea near Weston-super-Mare for a family picnic. Coming back, we stopped to give the children a ride on the ponies at Weston-super-Mare. Changing back into uniform I caught the 6.30 p.m. train back to London. It reached Paddington at 9 p.m. and I made my way to the Mall and Buckingham Palace. There was a good-tempered crowd calling for the King and Queen. They kept on coming out onto the balcony. I fell in with a crowd of service personnel celebrating and did not get back to quarters in Chelsea until 3 a.m. The scenes outside the Palace celebrating the 50-year anniversary of the Second World War reminded me of these past events. It is consoling and reassuring to find that the British still flock to the Palace on special remembrance days. It was moving to see the Queen Mother still coming out onto the balcony at the age of 95.

With the end of the Great War came a wave of dances and parties. Parents of marriageable-age daughters were looking for suitors but there were few men of the right age. For four long years 18- and 19-year-olds had led their troops 'over the top' from the trenches and been killed. A whole generation had been wiped out. I suspect politics and business affairs felt a lack of talent from the younger generation until the Second World War. I did not enjoy watching the older girls practically fighting over any eligible male. This kind of function came to a natural end quite quickly.

In 1919, we began a wonderful year for us all. Mother's young brother Berry had run away from school and enlisted underage in the army. He had suffered a knee injury and was demobbed early. He came to live with us and went to the Research Station for some agricultural training. Father was still up in London for part of each week doing some work at the Ministry of Food. Mother was delighted to have Berry as a companion while Father was away. They went to the theatre each week and at weekends there were parties both at home and at other houses in the village. Everyone was so glad the war was over. Berry loved the country-side; with him, the boys and I went bird-nesting the proper way, searching out the nests but then watching the birds hatch the eggs and dash hither and thither searching for food for their hungry offspring. We learned the names of flowers and trees, searched local streams and ponds for fish, knew where foxes lurked and watched rabbits playing till they scampered in fright to their burrows. He opened our eyes to the natural world. He teased and bullied us and was our little sister's ideal. It was a rewarding year that gave us all our lasting love of Nature.

The early 1920s was the era of the Bright Young Things. Their exploits and those of our much-loved Prince of Wales filled the gossip columns of newspapers. I was too young for this wave of parties and entertainments, but school friends had elder sisters and we listened hopefully to tales of happenings like progressive dinner parties – each course at a different house – and those hilarious treasure hunts. The girls dashed about in sports cars driven by dashing young men. My brothers had motorbikes by now. I did have rides to picnics on their or their friends' pillions as a consolation prize.

The General Strike came while I was doing School Certificate exams. With exasperation I watched the headmistress giving permission for VI form girls to join canteens to serve all the volunteers from university who drove buses, lorries and even trains. Why was I not old enough to take part?

At last the time came to leave school. It was decided, rather against the headmistress's plans for me, that I was to go to Leeds University to study textiles. What a decision! To throw over the chance to go up to Cambridge and read science, Father's choice, or to go to Oxford and read English, school's choice – good for the school noticeboard. My cousin was at Caius, brother Norman was to leave Clifton and spend a year in Grandfather's business before going up to Downing. I cannot imagine now how I stood firm in my choice. This was 1926, mine was the generation of schoolgirls that cut nine inches off our skirts when leaving school and going to university. It was a sudden change and felt wonderfully free.

3

Further Education

College authorities took no account of how many children a man had and there were five of us for Father to educate. I suppose I could have got an exhibition to Oxford to read English or Cambridge to read science because I was above average in my lessons. Curiously I took a very mixed Higher Certificate, main subjects, English and science, subsidiary language, Latin, Renaissance period, but there would not have been any money attached to these scholarships because of Father's income, although there were two boys very near me in age to educate as well. He was now Professor of Horticulture and Agriculture at Bristol University as well as Director of the Research Station. I did not want to go to university to read either English or science. I was already bitten by the art bug. I really would have liked to do dress design, but of course in a scientific family like that it was out of the question. However, I was determined to get to art school.

In the Easter holidays Professor Priestly, from Leeds University, who was Aubrey's godfather came down on some botany business and stayed with us as usual. When he heard the arguments about what was to be done with me when I left school he said, 'Well, Professor Barker, Leeds Textile Department is looking for a guinea pig and doesn't mind whether it is a boy or a girl. They want to have a student to train part-time at the art school and part-time at the university. Do you think you would like that?'

It was decided that I should go back to Leeds with Professor

Priestly, stay with them and have a look at the Textile Department and of course the art school. I settled for this plan, so in late September 1926 I went up to Leeds University. I was to live at Weetwood Hall. In the first days, finding it bitterly cold, I suggested to two other girls that we went looking for sticks as two of us had rooms which had fireplaces. In this way I made two friends who have lasted me almost until now.

Weetwood Hall was another of those houses which have influenced me. It had the date 1605 over its front door, but may have been earlier. The moulded plaster ceiling in our common room was decorated in strapped lozenges and rectangles in some of which were Catherine of Aragon's pineapple – her symbol. The old part had lovely shining parquet floors. There was some beautiful antique furniture about, which looked as if it might have been there for ever – chests and settles and tables. Our Warden, Mrs Redman-King, was very interested in the Impressionists so we had several good reproductions and some originals lent by the Vice-Chancellor, Sir Michael Sadler. She was also friendly with an artist named Jacob Kramer – she had obviously been given or bought some of his paintings – and there were two practically life-sized charcoal nude drawings, effectively framed, hanging in our dining room. When we had dances the student committee did not approve of these, although I thought they were beautiful. They said, could they be removed because we would be having supper in the dining hall? This really amused me very much but, of course, people were not quite so happy with bodies all over the place as we are today.

The grounds were beautiful, mature trees and sloping lawns and a home wood with bluebells massed under the trees – absolutely marvellous. I always enjoyed having two springs – one at home during the Easter holidays and a second one at the beginning of term when back at Weetwood, because in Yorkshire seasons were nearly a month later than in Somerset.

I visited Weetwood on my last trip to Leeds in 1992. I walked up the drive and looked for the last time, because they are spending a tremendous number of pounds – millions – in turning it into a sort of residential conference centre, highly luxurious, for the university. Probably they will ensure that those grounds which I loved so dearly will be beautifully kept up but I regret its loss as a home for students.

It was fortunate that the Sunday after attending the Textile Festival at Bradford, two years earlier, on the way home, I had gone out to Weetwood and it was still occupied by students, this time mature students from overseas. I introduced myself to the young warden and assistant warden and they said, 'Go round, explore, look up your old haunts.' So I was able to wander up and down. The grotto, where we had a pool with axolotls in, surrounded by several exotic palms and different greenery – which was, of course a favourite haunt for sitting out at dances in our day – had disappeared. The library had been moved downstairs and a new one built, probably on the site of the grotto. Mrs King's sitting room, which opened onto a terrace where Albert, our resident peacock, used to come to enjoy a chocolate while people drank their coffee after dinner, was now a students' common room. There was a big TV set, very noisy, and several large young men lying about on the couches and draped over the chairs. I thought, with rather shocked horror, how Mrs King would have hated to see her apartments used like this. However, I was sitting in the library finding some books which had been there in my day and having a sentimental look at them, when a group of four girl students came in, of all nationalities and various ages, and they said to me, 'The Warden says you were a student here, way back in the twenties. What was it like in *those* prehistoric days?' I was very happy to tell them, and although this was now spring, April or May, and it was warmer, they said that, yes, they too had suffered the intense cold, although now it was centrally heated. It was a real trip down memory lane and I loved it. I'm glad I had it then, if it is all going to be tidied up, made modern and spoilt.

To go back to my course. I spent three days a week at the university and two down at the art school. It was something and nothing for me at the art school. There was not time for me to go to life classes. I went to design and still life, but the emphasis was on the designing. At the university, as I was the first girl ever to be enrolled there in the textile department as a full-time student, I went to all the lectures, except business-economics and a language, possibly Spanish.

34

Certain differences, of course, had to be made in my programme and I was allowed more time in the handloom sheds, which quickly became my home from home. Percy Higgins was the overlooker for the long time that he was at Leeds. My 1992 visit was like going back home, to walk through the archway from the road and go into the sheds. I did powerloom weaving, of course, and loom study, cloth structure, cloth analysis, material study and, horror of horrors, knowledge of sheep, which the Professor took. All went swimmingly. We had lectures in the main lecture hall, which was tiered, quite a high one, from top to bottom. I was allocated a place on the left-hand side of the gangway, right down in front under the nose of the professor. It was not the done thing for any young man to come and sit beside me but my current friend of the moment would sit in the seat behind me and lean over to talk to me when the opportunity arose. When this went on too long, all the other young gentlemen would stamp loudly, which was a bit embarrassing! Then came one dreadful day when we were going to talk, or at least the Professor was, about sheep breeding! He marched in and said a few words from the platform and then leant over and addressed me. 'Miss Barker, we shan't be needing you this morning.' So I had to pack up my books and go, stamped loudly by all the men. Outside, in the hall waiting, was the lecturer in design, ready to tease me, because he knew that would annoy me. I was indignant. Dammit all, I'm a country girl and I have lived with farms and animals, I probably know as much about the practical side of sheep breeding as anyone, including the professor. I did not see why I should have to be barred, particularly as I would have to answer questions in examinations, but of course, this was the 1920s.

It was not all fun being the only girl among, I suppose, about 75 men. My fellow students were of all types: some lordly young gentlemen who had already been to Oxford or Cambridge, sons of mill owners who would be getting some practical work before they went into their fathers' firms; as were similar young gentlemen from all round the world; but it was leavened by a section of youngsters who had been very promising in their work at a mill, and who were being put through by the management on some sort of arrangement. Funnily enough, we all mixed in together quite happily but there was a certain feeling that I was privileged, because I had the same surname as the professor (it took quite a lot of convincing everybody that I was not a relative, and that my father was a professor too but of horticulture and agriculture). Anyway, I think it might have been an easier time if there had been another girl there with me.

Weavers will want to know a bit more in detail about what we actually did. The handloom shed was filled with looms. There were about six rows of ten looms each. Most of these were Dobbies of various capacities, probably the smallest of 8 shafts, 12, 16, 32, and there was one for 48 shafts. This is not the right place to explain how a Dobby works. You did have to prepare little wooden pegs on lags to show whether you wanted a shaft to be lifted or left in its resting position. All these shafts were attached to a harness and worked by this series of lags, which revolved in an endless chain around a cylinder at the top of the loom. This was turned over by stamping, and I say stamping because some of the Dobbies were pretty heavy to work, on a single treadle. There were two or three Jacquards and these were mostly ceded to me because on the whole my fellow students were not interested. They did not really want to go to the bother of doing a point paper design, cutting the cards from it, lacing the series of cards, and generally getting the Jacquard, which was a much more delicate instrument than the Dobby, to work. We had a good selection of yarns, in bins lining two walls, from the floor to the very high ceiling.

When I paid my last visit to the handloom sheds, just after the Bradford conference, I exclaimed with delight. This amused the loom tuner and the girl student who was helping him. My exclamation was caused by the fact that there were so many more yarns in brilliant colours than there had been in my day. The young gentlemen were very good at suitings, dull grey worsteds and herringbones. Sometimes an occasional tweed with perhaps a modest overcheck was designed as a variation. I found the neutral colours limiting for my sort of designing until a lecturer in the Dyeing Department next door gave me some of the new rayon to experiment with. This was true luxury and I really enjoyed it, although it was very tricky to use. We spoiled several hanks because we were not very good at winding the filament at the time.

I had a look around the looms on that recent visit to Theo Moorman's Memorial Exhibition in 1992 and sadly I do not really know that things have changed much, despite the brighter colours and the contemporary ingenuity of machinery there. Now there were 19 girls in the first year to one man, and that one man left at Christmas. In my day it was the other way round – 19 men to one girl. Now there were bright fabrics on the loom. They were a little bit ordinary, I felt. Perhaps it was unfair to judge the first year. Anyway, I was always very happy there and Percy Higgins, the overlooker and loom tuner, was always trying to find new cloth structures for me. I love cloth structure. William Watson's book *Textile Design, Part 1* and later *Part 2, The Advanced Textile Design,* was our bible. Cloth analysis I managed reasonably well. You sat with your little sample under strong electric light, you had a piece of glass that magnified and with two pins on little wooden holders, you solemnly dissected it row by row and copied down the overs and unders onto squared paper. Material study speaks for itself and we did have a wonderful selection of rare fabrics and yarns and fibres to learn from because of our professor's constant foreign travels in the long summer vacation.

I think the dyeing was the subject that seems most familiar still today. It has not changed very much. We dyed samples in a special sort of bath where six stainless steel little bowls were suspended, because we usually dyed a range of six colours, always, of course, in the pure colour, carefully weighed in the air-conditioned weighing room, brought in a container to dissolve on a little sheet of special paper. These bowls were heated from underneath; it was steam heat because that was constant and we could regulate it with a little tap. You fished about with your glass rod and after the allotted time you pulled out your samples and took them to dry. Soon, after we had become experts and done most of the ordinary dyestuffs then in use, we were taught match dyeing. This, of course, was more difficult and did depend on how true an eye you had for colour. Later, when I worked in a contract design studio in London, it became obvious that people see colour slightly differently, some see it warmer than it really is and some cooler. The head of the studio could reasonably decide whether the colour paint we had mixed (grinding it smooth on the glass slab and adding the right amount of gum) would match the chosen wool tuft so that the paper design would be true to the finished carpet.

Loom study was very important. We learnt to understand how all the looms, including the power looms, worked and we had to draw little diagrams to show different bits of the machinery. We also studied cloth finishing and had some practical experience in this which has been invaluable in my later life because understanding the principles means that, even in a rough and ready sort of homely way, you can get good results. The weave you cannot rival is worsted, and in the old days we used to be able to send anything we wove worsted fashion up to Leeds or Bradford to be professionally finished. It is the crabbing and the blowing where you need the specialities, and although Morfud Roberts devised a way it could be done by hand, it never seemed to me to rival what industry did. It irked me when I came back to teach hand-loom weaving several years later how people who were teaching there seemed so much to despise industry and machine weaving. I felt all my life that I never saw such skill as those loom tuners and handlers had in their hands, possibly inherited from their forebears because Yorkshire has been a textile place for many, many years. I think machine weaving just grew out of the original hand weaving. People were used to all the skills of spinning, their judgement of yarns and the tension, so they have inherited far more of the real textile skills than people who have just taken it up and not gone through the mill.

Now Women's Libbers may feel a little dismayed, but there was some doubt as to whether a girl would be capable of taking the end of term exams in my first year. After a few weeks and a look at what I had been doing, someone said, 'Better let her have a go.' I am happy to say that the results floored them all, for in most of the subjects I came out top and always with a high percentage of marks. I think the reason was that they were all completely new subjects to me and so therefore I paid attention to lectures. Also I had been to a good girls' school and I had

38

always been able to write fluently; my handwriting is childish but legible and quite decorative. I spell naturally and I do not make blots, and I think every one of my rivals suffered from one or other of these deficiencies. Also my diagrams must have been clear and pleasing because of the art school influence. Anyway, after that first term's results there was never any question that I should not do the full regime that the men did. I could not go on for a textile degree without staying longer than my three years, because I needed to add a language and business economics. So all I have is a Textile Diploma in Industry with my industrial design exams that I took at the art school.

Work at the art school was very different. Design class sat in a large room with windows down the two opposing sides. We sat at benches on which we propped our drawing boards. It was presided over by two dear ladies, pretty ancient to my eyes and I wondered how qualified they were. They did attractive calligraphy and things like that, but with the wider field of textile design, all they said was, 'Now you'd better have a book, dear,' – and trotted round and found the appropriate book.

The design teacher, a Mr Simpson, was well known for his church design locally and there came a time when we were set a project. We had to design three panels about a yard wide and two yards high. One was to be for church decoration, another was to be for a cinema (picture palaces, as they were then called), and the last was for a domestic interior. I think we were given a fortnight to complete this – what nowadays would be called a project. Well, I used a ruler to divide my space into three tall oblong panels and made complicated tracery, which again made full use of the ruler, and at the top I had about three compartments about half a yard square and in these I put a diamond and so arranged the tracery and the interlacing that they looked not unlike lilies. I did this in pale soft colours, greys, dull brown, a little grey-green and white. This came out top of the religious section, much to my amazement. For the cinema I had a low centre point and again I had an elongated diamond in, I think, bright yellows in my central panel, but I somehow contrived lines, this time coming out in circular fashion, over-lapping so that they made a whole scale-like pattern. These I did in brilliant colours, much in the order of the rainbow. This again was far more daring than anything my fellows did, but sadly in the domestic ones, mine was a complete flop. Mr Simpson shook his head sadly and said, 'I hope this doesn't prophesy the sort of life you are going to lead.' I think it might well have been a straw in the wind, because I certainly would not describe myself as domesticated.

During my first summer vacation, I had to stay on a month after the university went down, because the art school had a much longer term. I rather enjoyed living at Weetwood, not entirely on my own, because the Vice Warden was in residence and various visitors came. I felt that the gardens and the grounds belonged to me and I did sketching in the lovely summer evenings.

In this same vacation, the professor had been to Peru, and he came back next term with a wonderful collection of the llama wools, vicuna and other yarns in lovely natural shades, going from cream through the beiges and fawns to richer browns to a really dark brown. As I was the only one at the university attending the art school I was set to do the designs for these. Lengths were woven from my designs in a Peruvian manner, which I had somehow to concoct from the few examples available in books because they must have authentic motifs, though I could arrange them how I liked. These were woven in lengths on the power looms. They were sent to textile exhibitions in Prague and Madrid and thus in my second year I was shown in international exhibitions. The professor went so far as to have his lounge suite recovered in my upholstery material which had little lines of Peruvian birds walking up and down zigzag fashion on them – a black, grey, fawn and white background. These stripes were about an inch wide. I was a bit startled when I saw the finished result at a students' tea party but Mrs Barker (who was a dear little wispy woman and deaf) trotted round in an indomitable fashion after her energetic husband to all those strange countries where sheep and such-like animals abounded. I did wonder if she really minded about that suite being recovered in this startling design.

I still have a few framed, mounted samples of those Peruvian designs, and looking at them after a lifetime of experience in designing, considering that they were done so near the beginning of my training, I do not think they look too bad.

40

Years and years later, I spent about a fortnight in the Textile Department in one of my long summer holidays, when I heard that London Guild were sending about half a dozen weavers up for a week's course in the handling sheds. The Textile Department said to me, 'You'd better come too, Mary, because we may find it difficult to understand them.' I remembered how I and the nephew of someone in our village, when we first got to Leeds as students, could hardly understand a word that was said to us, so I agreed to come along. The group included Dorothy Wilkinson of the London School of Weaving, Hilda Breed, Mary Kirby, who wrote that excellent book, *Designing on the Loom*, Dorothy Wilmshurst and I've forgotten the other person. Dorothy Wilkinson, aged, and a really dyed-in-the-wool hand weaver, but with masses of charm, got on best. I didn't like to explain to the others that it was not so much what she did but her whole manner and the way she jollied them up. She really fitted in excellently.

I had to explain to the few members of staff still there besides the overlookers and loom tuners that yes, they were well-known teachers. The general opinion was, well they don't know much! So I had quite a job being tactful. That is why sometimes my colleagues have felt a little bit annoyed and uneasy with me as I may have had greater knowledge and skill because of Leeds University. I know Ethel Mairet, when I worked for her, was partly pleased that I could tell her any technical problem, solve it and give her the reasons for a lot that she did not understand. At times, although she welcomed the information, she was quite cross with me because I knew it, but as I grew to love her dearly and really look on Gospels as a second home, I did not mind in the very least. I just thought how lucky I had been to have that Leeds experience.

I did realise, with that London Guild course, that as the week wore on all my fellows began to appreciate, as I did, the terrific skill that the loom tuners and overlookers had, the way they handled yarns, the way they knew quality, the way they considered cloth, the way they said, 'Mmm that is woven too tight – you should have woven it so and so, because you really want to draw in, in the finishing (to shrink, in your words), to make a perfect cloth.' I have never forgotten the dictum that cloth, when it comes off the loom, is thready and bare and needs to have its character brought out by its finish and the sett of cloth regulated by the right amount of shrinkage. There are two shrinkages to be involved, relaxation shrinkage, when it comes off the loom, and wet finish, when it goes into water or steam. Both of these play an important function when setting the cloth so it will not move again.

4

My Life in London

My time at Leeds had ended in what seemed disaster. My friends all had degrees, awarded with great ceremony to candidates decked out in cap and gown. Most were continuing for a further year in education. Teaching was the most usual career for women then. Mine had not been a degree course so I only achieved a Diploma in Textiles Industries. This would in itself not have upset me but I had to stay up for a further month after the others had gone in order to sit the Ordinary and Advanced Industrial Design exams at the art school. Three major exams in one term proved to be too much for me. Unfortunately, there was a sudden thunderstorm towards the end of Part I Design. A freak rainstorm swept in through the open windows, spoiling the nearly finished work of those sitting beneath. We mopped up as well as possible but to no avail. I went home dispirited and exhausted to receive the news I had failed Industrial Design Part I. It did not really matter because I sat the exam next summer at Camberwell School of Art as an external student.

It was not an encouraging moment to begin a search for a job with news of the Wall Street Stock Market crash. However, with a little help from Leeds, I landed a job in the contract design studio of a famous carpet firm in London. It was to begin on 1 January 1930. It was arranged that I would live at Bedford House, a YWCA Hostel in Baker Street. (Years later it changed into the Sherlock Holmes Hotel. I visited it out of curiosity. The hotel building was still the same but the decor had changed unbelievably.) I booked a room for a fortnight, but stayed for nearly two years. I had a cubicle on the top floor of a mews annex. In the next one lived Marian Knight, who taught ballet at the Cone Ballet School, and Margaret Davidson, who worked in an office. We shared a skylight. It was bliss for someone brought up in the country that there was a fire escape overlooking the mews, where there were stables with real horses. We could sit out there among the roofs. In a room on the landing there lived Constance Faulkner, a student in catering at Debenhams. We became great friends. Con and I played bridge together and shared a love of books – Marian taught me to love ballet, while Dave and I got into all sorts of mischief together. The friends I made then were friends until they died. It is sad to survive all one's playmates but that is a price to be paid if one has a long life.

There was breakfast, which we collected cafeteria style, dinner was served to us at tables for eight. The YWCA partly financed their restaurant by serving lunches for workers around. On Sundays we got four meals a day and all for 25 shillings a week, plus or minus according to room. Dinner was soup, meat then pudding, served by maids. There was always milk pudding as well as stewed fruit or jelly or whatever. It was the custom of residents to say 'Both' to the maid's query about choice of pudding. Never having enjoyed rice puddings before, I learnt to like the Bedford House variety.

The studio where I worked was on the top floor of a building in Newgate Street. Our front door was round the corner in St Martins Le Grand. We were surrounded on two sides by Christ Church; but better than that, the studio looked straight down the ancient thoroughfare, Ivy Lane, that led to St Paul's. Halfway down on the right side was the Ship Inn, reputed to have been there in Queen Elizabeth I's reign. I did not know it then but later discovered that it was once owned by my great-uncle Fred. This whole area was swept away when the City rebuilt the bombing damage around St Paul's. I remember being taken to lunch at the Ship by my boss, and being fed on rare steak (which I have always hated) because he thought I was anaemic.

The first morning, I was given a 2 yard by 2 yard sheet of 10 by 10 squares to an inch and told to design as many of 9 inch by 9 inch square repeat patterns as I could in two colours, beige and brown. I was given a brush and a dish of paint. The patterns must repeat top and bottom and side by side. One idea led to another: a Chinese poem, then a strap pattern, regular small geometric figures, a Persian pine, a woodgrain, why not a type of parquet, and so on. By the next day they were all indicated. 'Oh,' said the boss, 'do they all repeat?' I had used strips of similar paper to prove this. I was then led to the slab, an old washstand covered with thick glass, and shown how to grind body colour till smooth with a palette knife and add gum arabic and water to make a smooth paste. He produced two tufts of wool, one dark brown, one a toning pale beige, and left me to match these in paint. I then went on to paint my patterns neatly. Various people came to look. No one said anything, but for the next few years, I kept recognising one or two of my repeat patterns as new stock was sent up from the factory.

The Studio Head Designer was a Greek, Basil Constantine Baltazanos, who had come to England as a young man and had married his landlady's daughter. He had thrown the javelin in the Olympic Games when they were held in Athens. He was a dictator in temperament, capable of hurling a stool around and throwing it across the studio when in a temper. He had a certain charm and on the whole was benevolent to the girls who worked for him. We were known as Mr Baltazanos' young ladies to differentiate us from the office girls who worked three floors below. The top floor, mostly studios, was reached by a very rickety lift, worked by a boy. It is pleasant to recall that he finished up as Officer Manager 20 years later. There were five girls working in the studios, painting in the designs, full-size, to go up to the factory. Two of them became lifelong friends, Mary Knight and Monica Smith.

The work consisted of providing designs for palaces, embassies abroad, hotels, cinemas and theatres at home. The Royal Opera House, Covent Garden, when redecorated in the 1930s, had a carpet in five shades of pinky red that had taken me a whole summer, six weeks, to paint in from Mr Baltazanos' design. There were Louis XVI-type swags of roses and other flowers, together with trophies of musical instruments.

Interior decorators would come to the studio with plans and

45

samples of interiors, needing carpets; it was trial and error to get the design to meet with their approval. We had textiles magazines from around the world, and because I could remember where a photograph on a page was, I was put in unofficial charge of these. Woe betide me if I could not locate an illustration needed in a hurry.

Sometimes we were sent out to museums to copy valuable ancient carpets, sometimes we were told to wander round shops to collect ideas. When we were not busy, we designed modern rugs. Once we were sent, all expenses paid, by the firm to see the International Show in Paris, where most countries had a pavilion.

We used to buy ham rolls for lunch three pence each, four if there was sliced tomato included, and a penny apple or banana for pudding. We worked from nine o'clock till 5.30 and only had a Saturday morning off once in a blue moon as a special treat. We had a saying, 'There isn't a man in the City happily married between the hours of nine and five, but after that, watch it, girls!'

Monica Smith and her sister at home had season tickets for the Prom Concerts at Queens Hall. When they were not going to use them, Monica wold give them to me for the evening for myself and hostel friends. I handed them back next morning at work.

Bedford House was often given theatre seats for first nights. Theatre managers like to have their stall and dress circle seats full. If you had evening dress, the management would give you two or even four tickets. We got to know the downstairs and the galleries of all the London theatres. The drill for gallery seats in those days was to put down a stool for sixpence in the queue in the morning on your way to work. You returned to the queue to sit on your stool at 6.30 p.m. and went in at 7 p.m. Later, for ballet at Covent Garden, the system was more complicated. A head of the queue was chosen – someone retired or out of work. You still put down your stools en route for work but one of your party must check in every four hours. During Colonel de Basil's Ballet de Russe de Monte Carlo, we went there most nights of the week.

To combat theatre fatigue, I went to golf lessons at Gamages and with Squeak (Ann) Williams, went out to Greenford public course on Saturday afternoons. Another country pursuit was to go out to Highgate to swim in the Kenwood Ponds; we would take a picnic on a fine Sunday.

After two years, Marian, Dave and I got tired of living at Bedford House. We found a flat to rent from a man who was sometimes an MP, then doing a spell as actor-manager at some little theatre outside London. This flat had good furniture, a delightful suite from Heals in the sitting room. Their charlady, Mrs Clarke, went with the flat to see that it was looked after properly, and became a dear friend. I visited her last towards the end of World War II.

We were the first generation of girls to live in flats in London. Most lived in clubs, hostels or with landladies in domestic digs. Not being sure of the way my family would look at this change, I waited until we had moved, then wrote home 'My address now is – !' Our new home rapidly became a refuge for all friends and family needing a bed for the night in London. This continued with all our subsequent flats.

The first flat was in Marylebone High Street. The front door of the block was between a tobacconist and wine shop and a public house called the Rose of Normandy. There was a legend that there had been an inn on this site from Norman times. The tobacconist turned out to be a fence and was connected with a famous robbery in which Regent Park Canal had to be dredged to recover booty. There was a ground floor flat under ours, number 1, then up a flight of stairs to the front flat, number 2, and our back one, number 3. Our front door opened onto a long passage lit by windows looking out over a flat roof with skylights belonging to the pub. This was always well lit and there was often the sound of music and laughter drifting up. The rooms opened off this passage, first a double bedroom with a window overlooking its counterpart in number 2, across the flat roof of the tobacconist; next was the sitting room, with a window looking east beside the fireplace, then came the kitchen, looking south, not as wide as the other two rooms, with a single bedroom where I slept. There was a loo at the end of the passage with a bathroom jutting out over the Rose. This had a deep but small square bath with a seat halfway up inside. Dave kept a bowl of goldfish she had won at a fair and she and I used to give them a swim in the bath when we changed the water each week.

We never got to know any of the other residents. One night the other two came and woke me up. They had seen three men on the wine shop roof. We watched, and sure enough the men ran carefully along the wall about a yard away from my bedroom window. This wall bordered a back alleyway and this would enable them to get into a house in the next street. Police knocked at our front door and we showed them the escape route.

The rent of the flat was £3 per week, leaving us 15 shillings for housekeeping. At first we took it in turns to do the housekeeping for a week each but soon found I was best at this task, rarely getting into debt and could provide the most interesting diet. Dave and myself often ran out of money, no shillings for the electric meter, so we wrapped ourselves in our eiderdowns on Thursday evenings – wages were paid on Fridays – and sat on our front doorstep, using the staircase light to write our weekly letters home, waiting for the wealthy Marian to come in to feed the meter. In those days Marylebone High Street was almost like a village street; I knew the grocer, the baker and the butcher, and years later after we had left that district, I went back in WRNS uniform to the grocer and all the staff came out to look at me with touching pride.

We lived there for three years until Robert, our landlord, got another seat in Parliament. Robert gave us strawberry and cream teas on the terrace and took us round the Houses of Parliament. Dave had to go home to look after her father as her mother had died. Marian and I went to a mews flat in Portman Mews North. Our front door was round the corner in a side branch of the mews where there were stables for the United Dairy ponies. We could hear them kicking their stalls below our bedroom, which had a skylight. This flat was unfurnished so we had to buy some furniture. I have some of it still.

Living in the mews was bliss. There was a garage halfway along, open all night. We nicknamed the nightwatchmen there Daddy Offord and Joe Offord. One of them was always on duty at nights and would see us safely home if alone. One night I had come back from some May Week party at Cambridge on the midnight trail. Joe saw me to the corner, I opened the front door, did not switch the light on, ran up the stairs and someone leapt up and grabbed me. I reached back for the switch, screaming with fright, and saw my assailant was a young policeman, sneaking a sleep on our stairs with his helmet off. Joe rushed back and gave him a sound ticking off.

We were friendly with the grooms too; they called us each morning with our milk. We left our front door open after Percy Sydney and his family left the other flat over the double garage below. Percy Sydney was our landlord's chauffeur and drove the Rolls Royce, another smaller sporty car and his own battered Morris. We did not like his wife or baby and were glad when they left for a house, but Percy was a charmer and I had quite a romance with him.

Opposite there was a line of mews houses, at the bottom of the long gardens belonging to the big houses lining the north side of Portman Square. The one opposite our flat belonged to an old lady. A door had been cut in the coach house long doors and we never knew if it would be the coachman, his wife or the horse that would step out. They were a comic couple and we christened them Jack Hulbert and Cicely Courtneidge after the actors. Every afternoon, Jack brought out the horse, harnessed him to the brougham and drove round to the big house to see if the lady wanted to drive round the park. If she did not wish to go on this outing, Jack returned to pick up Cicely.

While we were living here, King George V and Queen Mary had their anniversary and drove round London. The whole group of mews residents cheered them as they drove along Baker Street.

British history has many examples of lively Princes of Wales who have become excellent kings when they finally came to the throne. Take Henry V, Charles II, or Edward VII, for example. The British public took a tolerant line on their love lives, provided they were conducted with proper decorum. There seemed no reason why our Prince of Wales, who had been such a golden boy on his travels promoting Britain round the world, would not follow their example, but we had reckoned without Mrs Ernest Simpson, an American with a second husband. There was plenty of gossip and I actually saw them together at the

Chelsea Flower Show. She was quite plain, very neatly dressed with black hair drawn back from her face and looked animated and amusing.

King George V died and we had a new King. Mrs Simpson took a fancy to become Queen. The Prime Minister, Mr Baldwin, rightly took the view that the public would not stomach the lady as Queen. The Royal Family, headed by Queen Mary, was appalled. The new King insisted that he could not live and reign without the woman he loved. He abdicated and his brother, the Duke of York, had to ascend the throne as George VI. He had an excellent wife, Elizabeth, now the beloved Queen Mother, who was a tremendous support to him. He had a stammer and was a quiet shy individual but did his duty, and with the coming war, became a splendid King. When his elder daughter Elizabeth became Queen, he was truly mourned. The Duke of Windsor, once Edward VIII, attended the funeral, and I for one did not recognise the tired, sad, worried, elderly man as our once popular Prince of Wales. A case of the world lost for love is an impracticable dream.

Eventually the mews garage, flats over and the stables were sold to developers to build small town houses. Our landlord paid us £100 for the surrender of our lease. We then moved back to Marylebone to a block over the butcher's back premises in the High Street. It was here one Sunday in 1938 that a man brought gas masks for us. We moved again further out to a top floor flat in West Hampstead, but we only occupied this one for three months before war was declared and my wonderful colourful London life was over. Just a memory of happy times.

No one could work in the City and be unaware of the darkening clouds of war. The threat was there; possibly this threw my happy lifestyle into colourful contrast. Ballet at Covent Garden in the summer. Winters devoted to opera. The gallery there seemed like home. We used to rush for seats in the gallery on the right-hand side, looking down on the stage. Loud music and robust singing used to affect me, Wagner used to make my nose bleed, but I used to lie happily in the passageway, flat on my back, mopping away. With the interval the flow stopped. Then there was Sadlers Wells, the glory of the Markova/Dolin *pas de deux* in *Swan Lake* and Markova's special ballet, *Giselle*. The shock when Alicia abandoned Ninette de Valois to form a ballet company with Dolin. The excitement when young Peggy Hookham was translated from the chorus to Markova's star roles and christened Margot Fonteyn. It was a daring move by Ninette that paid dividends for the next 40 years. At first, balletomanes tended to say that it was because she fitted the costumes but Margot soon proved she could dance. Frederick Ashton was always a help to her. Another Sunday evening treat was Madame Rambert's Ballet company at the Mercury. Star performances here were *Façade*, William Walton's ballet with verse spoken by Edith Sitwell and the polka danced by Markova. Another ballet at the Mercury was *Bar Aux Folies Bergères* with beautiful Pearl Argyll as the Barmaid and Markova the Goulu. Another favourite was *Jardin Aux Lilacs*, with its dancers floating out into the scented garden from the Imagined Ball, one of Antony Tudor's outstanding suggestive creations. Sometimes the symphonic ballets of Massine suggested what was to come: the red line of mourning women led by Nina Verchinina in the second scene of *Choreartium* (Brahms' Fourth Symphony) or Lichine confronted by Fate in *Les Presages* (Tchaikovsky's Fifth Symphony). *Job* was a powerful ballet by Ninette de Valois and she also gave us a poignant role for Markova in the *Rake's Progress*.

Life was extremely hard for the increasing number of unemployed in the 1930s – the Welfare State had not yet dawned. The plight of the Jarrow miners as they marched through the City to the Guildhall, unshaven, with ragged clothes and soles flapping on worn-out shoes, touched our hearts and we girls emptied our purses of hard-earned cash into their caps, they looked so tired and hopeless and dirty. The memory of this march and the contrast of the later one in the 1980s, all in their neat matching anoraks, comfortably fed, with church halls etc. to sleep in and presumably with their unemployment money in their pocket, hit me hard. Life is never fair.

My personal life was changing too. My mother died at Cambridge in June 1937. She had been getting more disabled for years. At the age of 17 when she met my father, who was five years older than herself, she had a nervous breakdown. At that

51

time it was put down to the fact that she was a pupil-teacher at her old school, busy at home looking after the children, while her mother recovered from yet another miscarriage or pregnancy, and gadding about with Father. Later it was thought that this was the first sign of that dread disease, then named Desseminator Sclerosis of the Locomotor Nerves.

I can remember two mothers, one the lively dark girl, full of fun, always popular with many, many friends, the other an invalid, slowly but surely becoming worse, until she lay like a log, waited on hand and foot. The disease let up when she was pregnant. My youngest sister Anne was born in June when I was 14 years old. Mother had been quiet and not very mobile for months before the birth but then enjoyed good health until the following spring. The house was being redecorated, then Mother fell ill and specialists were called in. She recovered, but from that time it was downhill.

She had a series of companion-chauffeuses, she played bridge until she could not hold her cards. Father spent a fortune on specialists and treatment but all to no avail. At 17 years old, my sister Peggy gave up training at the children's hospital and stayed home to run the house for a few years, until Mother went into a nursing home and was eventually moved back to Cambridge, where she died. Father moved to the Director's House at the Research Station, selling our home to Mrs Round, the mother of Aubrey's great friend Ben. Peggy married Ben in the spring of 1938 and Father married Alicia Maunsell in June, a year after Mother's death. My step-mama was two years older than myself. It was not an easy situation; Aubrey and Anne were still living at home, so Anne was sent to Bristol University at least a year too young. It was a relief on the home front when war came. Alicia eventually had a girl, Shirley, in 1943, who rejoiced in being a half-aunt at the age of one month to Peggy's son Christopher. Father retired at the end of the war and after a few years bought a girls' boarding school for Alicia to run. This school, Westwing, gave him a happy well-looked-after old age. He had always enjoyed teasing us all and continued this from kindergarten to the senior girls.

To return to 1937, life went on, perhaps the theatregoing became more feverish. There were wonderful exhibitions to visit

52

and I went abroad on holiday with friends, but all the time, change seemed to threaten. Munich and Neville Chamberlain's 'Peace in our time' seemed to cancel each other. War was going to come, but not before the harvest was gathered in. Winnie, my college friend of old, and I watched the cornfields of France anxiously as we travelled south by train to Biarritz. I did one of my faints – anxiety complex? – but recovered quickly, aided by the ministrations of two capable nuns. One day someone from the embassy called at our hotel. We British were mustered and told that France had ordered mobilisation. We were to stay put until the embassy gave the word. The railways must not be clogged by civilians.

We went by bus to spend the day at a village up in the hills, looking down across the river to Spain. We quickly realised what a mistake this was. A line of coaches filled the main street. They had come to collect all the young men of the neighbourhood to transport them to the railway. Families had turned up in force to say goodbye. They felt they might never see their sons and brothers again. Sweethearts wept uncontrollably. For the elders, this scene was a repeat performance of the one 25 years before in 1914. We crept away feeling guilty and had our picnic. As we waited for the bus back to Biarritz at the local inn, the innkeeper, a middle-aged man with a limp, shrugged his shoulders and murmured, '*C'est la guerre,*' as he served us our drink.

After three days, the embassy official came back at dinner-time – make for home as quick as you can, was his message. Other English people at our hotel had travelled out first-class, some transferred to wagons-lits. Winnie and I were running out of money, we had packed our suitcases and sent them home 'luggage in advance'. We decided to return as we had come, third-class; we had just a small carrybag each and on the way to the station we bought rolls, ham, cheese, fruit and drink for the journey. It was slow – it took 12 hours – and Paris was dark when we got there. They had turned the street lighting off, there were no taxis for hire, the main routes were blocked by cars laden with people, luggage, even furniture strapped to the roof, all trying to leave Paris. What were we to do? We decided to walk from the Left Bank to the small hotel near the Gare Du Nord where we had originally booked for a weekend in Paris. I knew Paris better than Winnie and thought I could find the way. We crossed the bridge over the Seine, walked across the Tuileries garden, found the route to the Opera, then went straight up one of the boulevards. The difficult part was identifying the small road where the hotel was situated. It was shut; we banged at the door for ages. When it opened up they looked at us with amazement. They agreed to let us have a room. We needed food. They had none, but they rang a little restaurant in the same street, and they gave us a scratch meal. Next morning, we walked round to the Gare Du Nord to get the train to the coast. Was I glad to leave Paris. I had never seen a city in panic before.

It was a nightmare journey back on the boat, with people standing crammed together on all the decks. It was foggy and the fog-horns did not help. We disembarked calmly and took the train to Victoria. London was lit up, everyone seemed normal; people were carrying their small gas mask parcels, but that was all. We made our way to a friend in Richmond to collect the key of Winnie's flat. They gave us much-needed baths and a bed for the night. We slept until lunchtime after spending the evening making our hosts laugh over our adventures. I went back to our flat in West Hampstead the next day, Sunday, via Victoria. I remembered our luggage and called at the office. There it was safe and sound. On Monday morning, I went to work as usual. Once there, I told my adventures and made our elevenses. There was no work so the firm gave us a holiday until further notice. I decided to go to stay with my godmother in Cambridge and help with the children's evacuation.

Aubrey, Alice, Peggy and Ben were holidaying on the Norfolk Broads. My other brother, Norman,was in contact with them by telephone and I arranged to join them at the weekend, when the children would have been settled. They would pick me up at Yarmouth.

5

World War II

I walked along the quay at Yarmouth and found the yacht with only Peggy on board; she said the others had gone to find blackout material as Aubrey had heard the Germans were dive-bombing individual peasants working in the fields in Poland. They came back with some sheets of black paper that we cut to fit the portholes then set sail for Ranworth.

This small broad is delightfully sheltered; the village runs down to the quay. A little way up the hill is a small church with famous wall paintings. The next morning, Sunday, we walked up to the church, well before morning service. The Vicar greeted us, 'Have you got a wireless on board?' We said we had and he advised us to go back and turn it on at 11 a.m. as the Prime Minister was to make a speech. He was busy fixing his set-up in church so that his congregation should hear the broadcast. I had a hasty look at the wall paintings and we hurried back to our boat. Alice made coffee and we sat around the cockpit, turning the wireless full on. The Prime Minister announced that war had been declared on Germany and made a short speech. The evacuee children clustered on the quay, listening too. Then suddenly there was the sound of sirens – the air raid warning was given. The children ran back to their billets except for two brave little ones who decided that they would rather go home and be 'bombed up' with their mum and dad than stay in this dreadful place where people gave them grass (sliced beans to you and me) to eat. There was only one road out of Ranworth so as soon as it was discovered they were absent, someone got out his car and found them two or three miles away.

We cooked lunch discussing what to do. Finally, the boys decided that, as the boat was not due back at the boatyard till Saturday, we might as well finish the holiday. At first it seemed eerie as all the other yachts had returned to base but we soon got used to the solitude. No crowds of merrymakers, no noisy motor-boats, just an occasional fisherman. Wild life abounded; ducks, moorhens, even swans, accepted our presence. The weather was perfect. How lucky it was to enjoy peace and quiet on the Broads. At sundown, we blacked out our yacht and settled down to play cribbage. I would sometimes creep out on deck to watch the moonlight reflected in the water. A blissful week followed.

Early Saturday morning, the yacht was returned to the yard and we drove to Cambridge to see Norman at the factory. Then the others went on to Bristol while I took a train for London and our empty flat. Marian had already been sent with the ballet school to the country. My firm still had no work for us so we were put on half pay and sent home.

I gave up our flat, moved the furniture into store in Bristol and went home to the Director's House. I realised I must take up warwork and enrolled at Skerry's for a shorthand, typing and bookkeeping course. Pamela Henderson, a Captain RN's daughter, was a fellow pupil waiting to join the WRNS. After a week she disappeared and there came a message that I was to go for an interview with Chief Officer Bell. I went and was offered work on the naval ledgers. It would mean joining the WRNS but she assured me I would never have to wear uniform or do drill. A few months later uniforms from World War I arrived. Pam and I were suitable in size, so we were dressed up in them. After being shown to the Captain, I went into the Pay Office to show the naval writers. They wept with laughter at my umbrella skirt and floppy Girl Guide hat and promptly christened me their 'orphan child'.

The Captain decided our kit must be modified so we were sent to a good tailor who certainly turned out respectable little suits. Nothing could be done about the hairy serge. When it rained on our cotton hats, the dye ran and we would have navy blue partings in our hairstyles. This continued until our saucy caps were introduced a year or so later. By then I was a petty officer and had a velour tricorn.

The ledgers proved interesting. We worked in duplicate. A naval writer sat one side of the table, a Wren sat opposite, documents came first to the writer. After he had made his entry, he threw the piece of paper opposite to his partner. The Wren had to keep an immaculate ledger as at the end of the quarter, they were sent to the Director of Navy Accounts. These ledgers were entitled Rough for the writers, Fair for the Wrens. I was quickly promoted to Rough and happily scribbled notes over mine; my Fair was a young naval writer. He dropped blots of ink and his figures and writing were almost illegible. So it was decided my pencil notes must be rubbed out and my ledger sent in. Our unit was part of DEMS, Defensively Equipped Merchant Shipping, and our seagoing ratings – hostility-only volunteers in the early days of the war – were an individual bunch of men.

One had 400 names as a ledger. As names dropped out from death or disastrous wounding, or being set for a commission, new names were added from the following rough ledger. Being stationed in Bristol, we were often visited by men serving on ships in coastal waters. This provided human interest in the ledger work. It was the story of a man's life: his behaviour, fines for being drunk or other crimes, his love life, the names of his wife and children, and any other mothers of his children. We quickly discovered the truth about sailors having a wife in every port. The Lords Commissioners at the Admiralty held the view that it was the female who kept up Gunner So-and So's home that should have the marriage allowance. This involved close questioning and a freedom of arriving at the best answer. I found this both interesting and enlightening and became an expert. We had one coastal seaman who had four establishments at different ports. He was christened the 'Great Lover' by the Pay Office. Officers shook their heads over him but I took an interest, and by sorting out the ages of his various offspring, decided the problem. When the said sailor came in to see us, he proved to be a wizened little man, in no way the glamour boy we had imagined.

Another problem was that merchant ships travelled the world.

Our sailors went with them and, unfortunately, besides getting their meagre pay from the master of their ship, could call at any port, see the usually young naval officer and draw £5. Some became expert at this. All bills eventually came home to their name on our ledgers, and once the war was two or three years old, that name became a financial calamity. I became expert on the telephone at chatting up these officers round the world, warning them against being too generous to certain names.

Survivors presented problems, too. They were interviewed at the port of return and sent home or to hospital. They next needed to find out their pay. I shall always remember my first survivor. He had been into the Pay Office very early on – very worried as on his first trip on a coaster in the North Sea it was dive-bombed. He manned their sole gun and found that he could not work it. The master, not unnaturally, was annoyed and swore at him. I said consolingly to this tale, because he seemed an older, worried little man, that he had better ask to go on a liner or some other large ship which would have many ratings and even an officer on board, so he could learn to work the armament. He followed my advice and was posted to the ill-fated *City of Benares*, which was torpedoed in the Atlantic ferrying a cargo of evacuated children to Canada. No survivors. I sighed and pencilled in 'Missing Presumed Dead' against Stanley Albert's name. A few weeks later who should walk into the office but the missing man, Stanley Albert himself. We gave him a hero's welcome and all gathered to hear his story. When the ship sank, he had jumped into the sea, wearing his life jacket. After bobbing about for a few hours, he found an empty raft. He climbed aboard happily and for three days floated around enjoying the victuals and survivor kit, but then the raft came within reach of a ship's boat. The survivors were Lascar seamen, one white woman and several children. He was loath to leave his raft but did not like the lady being alone with the foreign seamen and the children, so reluctantly he climbed aboard. The children died one by one, the Lascars drank sea water and went mad, throwing themselves overboard. They drifted for three weeks before being picked up, rations long exhausted, and Stanley Albert was the sole survivor. He was returned to Liverpool and hospital then given leave. Unluckily, no one took note of his name and address and informed his relatives. He was still marked as missing. He owned a small greengrocer's shop quite near our 'ship' in Bristol. When he walked in, his wife and family were conducting a wake for him. They had decided he must be dead. This hurt him more than his dreadful adventure. Eventually we had to invalid him out.

This was 1940. News was bad – I had been out to lunch and went into our common room, switched on the wireless for the one o'clock news and heard the announcer, Stuart Hibbert, say, 'France has fallen.' There was Dunkirk, the 'phony' war was over. Air raids became nightly events. I was still an immobile Wren commuting from home.

One night we had a tremendous bomb in the field by the Director's House. Father and Alicia were out at the back, fire-watching. Anne and I were in the drawing room; she was drying her hair. I heard the noise of the 'rushing train' and shouted at her to take cover; picking up our spaniel, Whisky, I crawled under the grand piano. Soot poured down the chimney over her wet hair. Well trained, I asked, 'Where are the Mackintosh bags? I must go out and collect what is left of Pa and Alicia.' When I got out there, they were rushing in, dazed with shock. The bomb had exploded so near that the damaging debris had blown over the house. The fire watch came dashing up the long drive from the Research Station expecting to find disaster. We had forgotten the blackout and were making tea.

The next day, I came back a little early from work. The car was in the drive with my precious tapestry frame on top of it. I dashed into the house shouting, 'What are you doing with my tapestry?'

Alicia came downstairs lugging our fur coats. 'Oh,' she said, 'can't you read? There's a notice at the bottom of the drive. We have an unexploded bomb as well!' They had evacuated to the Research Station and as Winston Churchill was coming to tea, Alicia had come back to collect her best tea service and pick up anything of value. We slept quite comfortably and next morning, Sunday, there was a shout from the front and I dashed over to see the bomb explode. This time there were several holes in the roof.

Bristol suffered three devastating massive raids. It was time for HMS *President III* to move because of our precious records.

We went to Windsor and Eton. The Wrens were to live in Hodgson House, opposite the chapel, and work at Dedworth Manor, a mile out of Windsor. These were two interesting houses for my collection, but sadly I never drew them. Soon I added Clewer Park – a grand estate owned by an old lady who had been a favourite of King Edward VII. In the drawing room there hung a superb portrait of her reclining in a gorgeous white evening gown nursing two King Charles spaniels, with a third leaping up at her skirt. She lived alone in part of the house with her ancient retainers – two maids and a butler. In the grounds was the dog bungalow, where the 'Dog Lady' lived with 40 of these spaniels. Favourites were allowed to visit their owner for a few days.

My time at Hodgson House was one to remember. We were packed tight in uncomfortable quarters. The first night three petty officers slept on the floor in a study-bedroom that would normally have been occupied by one boy. Washing facilities were a line of basins under windows that looked directly out to those next door. There were three enormous baths, one in a room, the others on a landing under a skylight; there was never enough hot water to fill them.

A few days later more beds arrived, and we had a double bunk and single bed and I produced a curtain to cover our spare clothes. The WRNS officers lived in the master's part of the house with the naval officers. I was now Chief Wren and had to arrange fire watches and other duties. Naval writers shared the watchkeeping in a small office. They brewed tea continuously, but there was often a cup of black tea – i.e. Guinness stout – there for Chief Barker. I was having a delicate spell at the time, very run down and anaemic.

Each morning I had to muster the Wrens and count them aboard our bus to go to Dedworth Manor. The officers sat in the front seats, of course. We had an invalided-out ex-Guard as a driver. I had to give the command 'All aboard, Jack, shove off forward', and then leap on myself. Eton regarded this as a terrific joke. At first the boys did not care for the navy in their midst. However, once the Admiralty sent our gunnery bus down from HMS *President*, all fitted out with the smaller guns we put on ships, with an instructor to show the Wrens how to fire them, the boys began to take an interest.

Eton itself was welcoming; they lent us their parade ground for drill, we were free to go to services in the chapel and allowed to take out their smaller boats on the river. We had an enthusiastic concert party and our bus used to ferry us round the county in the blackout, doing shows in village halls. Pop was across our yard in Hodgson and the boys even took me over the premises. I was suitably impressed. They invited me to help with their entertainments, painting scenery and designing costumes and I was taken to one Breaking-Up Ceremony. When I left, I felt almost an Old Etonian.

Air raids continued; the drill was to carry out a table to the yard, I climbed on to this and Mary Francis held a torch to shine on the muster list. As I called Wren names, they went to shelter. Absentees' names had to be checked in officers' quarters to see who was on leave or had a pass out for the evening.

Eventually some of us moved out to Clewer Park, which was an Edwardian house in lovely grounds coming down to a tributary of the Thames and adjoining Windsor Racecourse. It had been built by King Edward VII for the current lady friend, Mrs Moss Cockle.

We walked to the manor one mile away, then back and forth at lunchtime, then home when work was over. It was a mile and a half into Windsor, a lovely walk in the blackout. We had to meet at a pub for the walk home. Drill now became an unwelcome duty for me. I had to form fours with the Wrens and dress the line, impossible as females either bulge forward or behind unevenly. We went on route marches down the country lanes. Agony when we met a detachment of Guards. The officer would salute and give the men the order 'Eyes right'. The Wrens would giggle; more embarrassment for me.

Windsor Castle was home to the King and Queen and their two daughters, Elizabeth and Margaret. The castle rang one day to ask if Elizabeth could join our Sea Rangers, she was old enough, but Margaret was only allowed to sit by and watch until they played games, when she was allowed to join in. This meeting took place one evening per week in the castle. There was always a tennis

61

table set up in the hall that had to be moved. One leg fell off and Margaret said that that always happened when Daddy moved it. A homely picture of palace life. Princess Marina, the Honorary WRNS Commandant, and the Queen inspected us at Dedworth. We had special services at St George's Chapel and the Wren petty officers had to take the collection; one more worry for me.

Clewer had splendid stables and let them to the owners of horses that were running in the races at Windsor. We used to visit them the evening before and watch the grooms petting the highly strung ones. The contrast the next day when a horse came back triumphant having won his race was a pleasure to see. This encouraged my love of racing. I do not bet but enjoy watching on television. It is an art of movement akin to ballet.

Dedworth Manor itself – well, it was so altered by our being there, all the rooms were used as pay offices, and one or two bathrooms were used for special things such as, say, naval records. It had, however, been beautiful, surrounded by polo grounds and tennis courts. We dug up some of the lawns for allotments and those of us who had any gardening skills tried to grow vegetables.

Most of the original girls who were there when I joined up were now officers. I was always delicate and the Medical Officer would not pass me as medically fit, but suddenly we got a new Medical Officer and he said if I gave up smoking he would pass me as fit because I would have less stress and be more comfortable living as an officer. It was near the time for my test. I was heading the long lines of Wrens in pay parade, a formal ritual which took place once a fortnight. The naval writers parade first. The Paymaster sat at his desk. With the Lieutenant Commander supervising, the rating stepped forward, saluted and laid his cap on the desk, and the pay was slapped on to it. He picked it up, saluted, turned and marched off. Their parade was near to finishing. I felt deadly faint. I hissed to the petty officer behind me, 'Carry on,' stepped forward, managed a smart salute and marched off down the passage. The secretary's office was on the right – she was an old chum from Bristol days . She told me later I opened the door and fell flat. There was an adjoining walk-in stationery cupboard. She seized my legs, dragged me in, shut the door and rang for the Medical Officer. I came round to see him climbing in through the window. A minute later the Lieutenant Commander arrived on the scene. He ordered the Medical Officer to bring his car round. They lifted me out through the window and he took me back to Clewer, where I was put to bed. I feared my test would fail, but no, within a week I was off to Greenwich.

Greenwich was a breathtaking experience. The sheer beauty of the two great parallel buildings, King Charles and Queen Anne, stretching down to the Thames, the Painted Hall for our meals bridging the gap, the chapel, where in the month I was stationed there we had both a wedding and sadly a funeral. It was as grand and historic as the castle and school at Windsor. Mary Francis and I went up together. Unluckily, after a quieter spell, air raids had become worse again. The Wren contingent were quartered in Queen Anne. The first night, the sirens sounded, officers rapped us awake in our cabins and we were marshalled down to the shelters, long tunnels that ran under the river, cold and damp. After a disturbed night down below, it was found that Queen Anne had had firebombs on the top floor. Several Wrens had lost both cabin and spare uniform. We all had to share what shirts etc. we had. As we had to appear trim from top to toe, correctly kitted out, this was a tragedy for some until Naval Stores came to the rescue. Hat with brown leather gloves was worn when we went in squads around the compound, the only extra allowed, our gas mask satchels.

Each morning we paraded in Queen Anne Quadrangle for a short service. The WRNs officer staff were there in force, but there was one first officer with fluffy white hair and woolly white dog who was always panted in late. This was Violetta Thurston, who together with many distinguished men, lectured us daily. She was brilliant on her subject, the Middle East. She knew of my textile background and got me into trouble keeping me after lights out looking at all her samples. Colour sergeants marshalled us, drilled us mercilessly and took our squad across the parade ground at the double.

One day, a paymaster captain was lecturing us on pay. He paused, stared out of the window across the grounds to King Charles Wing. We looked too and saw swastikas painted black on white circles as a German plane swooped down, its bomb doors opening, followed by the sound of explosion and the end of the building collapsing. 'I see nothing, ladies. Shall we continue?' he said.

Twenty-four Wrens sat terrified and trembling as we feverishly took down notes. In a minute or two, a WRNS officer rushed up and said 'Excuse me, sir, the young ladies should be in their shelter.' A short time later, the all clear sounded and we were marched over to lunch in the Painted Hall. The duty watch were absent, clearing the rubble. Tragically the Commander who taught us navigation was in bed with flu in King Charles and was killed. The colour sergeants included slow march in our drill and three days later we marched in the funeral procession from the chapel to the wharf, where the coffin was loaded onto a vessel to be taken out to sea for burial.

A day or two later our uniforms were finished and we were commissioned Acting Third Officer WRNS, and drafted to our posts. Mine was at the naval base in Milford Haven. This was quite intimidating. One of my duties was to take half a dozen sailors and a petty officer to the bank each morning to collect several thousand pounds in cash. I had to sign for it, see the sailors carry it and when we got back to the naval base, check that it was the correct amount. There were both bundles of notes and bags of coins. Our Pay Captain RN retired but recalled for the war had been on China Station. He was a martinet and ruled the Pay Office with a rod of iron. A Lieutenant RN paid the sailors at the base. I was sent out to the naval outposts with their pay.

Every officer at the base had to be Duty Officer for the Port one night in turn. I had not been there more than a week when my turn came. I was terrified, and as it happens I had an eventful night. A Colour Sergeant Royal Marine was my right-hand man – in fact he told me what to do. Under his guidance, I consigned drunks to cells, dealt with sailors' fights, mopped up their injuries until a sickbay rating arrived, and was beginning to enjoy myself. The haven was full of every sort of ship; most allowed their naval ratings ashore on leave. A storm blew up. I had to order the storm cones to be hoisted and organise parties of base personnel to go round all the pubs and dance halls to rout out the sailors and get them back to their liberty boats to return to the parent ship before the sea got too rough. An unpopular move. In the midst of the turmoil, the Pay Captain turned up to make sure I was taking the right action. Fortunately he found all in order.

After one month, I was drafted back to a DEMS post at Cardiff as the two WRNS Officers there were being posted overseas. I was junior to the Captain's new secretarial Second Officer. She turned out to be a disaster, both at the naval base and at WRNS quarters. The Captain DEMS sent for me, asked if I could manage the work and appointed me his PA Secretary as well as Paymaster for DEMS Bristol Channel Area. Luckily HMS *President III* had prepared me well. Captain Glossop, RN, was a retired destroyer captain who had been recalled for the war. He was a popular officer, his cap always at a jaunty angle, local Justice of the Peace and Lord of the Manor, in civilian life, popular with all ranks. So Cardiff was a happy posting and I stayed there until the war ended.

After demobilising our sailors and convoy signal-men, I went back to HMS *President III* at Chelsea in summer 1946. Here I was quartered in the Sitwells' house in Swan Walk, a most delightful house looking over the old Physic Garden. Our cabin was below the attic where William Walton had written his music before the war. One more move a short distance away to a house on the Embankment, where our cabin overlooked Chelsea Gardens, the home of the Chelsea Flower Show. Then I was demobilised and went to Hornsey College of Art.

The war years were a time to rejoice, a time to despair, a time to hope and a time to die. This brought out the right spirit in most people. Human nature was at its best. We were all in it together. The D-Day celebrations in 1994 and the commemoration of peace in 1995, 50 years on, showed this. The youngest recruits must by now have been 68 years old. The wonder was that so many young people joined in the rejoicing. Their grandparents and parents must have succeeded in describing their past. I am glad to have lived in that time but please God do not let it happen again.

6

Ethel Mairet

At last I was demobbed and lived for a little while with friends. After that my home was a funny first-floor best bedroom in a little semi-detached house. It overlooked a big house with the Mount View Theatre in its garden. This had a pleasant tree, and I used to look longingly across the road at it. Then I moved over to Highgate and lived in a beautiful house with a lovely garden down Hampstead Lane, before moving to 119 Hornsey Lane, which was late Victorian, again with a special garden. Somehow I always seemed to manage to live near beautiful gardens – or something lovely to look at.

Before the Second World War, as I have recounted, I worked at a carpet contract design studio in London. This studio looked down Ivy Lane to St Paul's past the famous Old Ship Inn, which once had belonged to my great-uncle Fred. The ivory tower world of the studio was compensated by the richness of that 1930s London world; opera, ballet, concerts, theatre, art exhibitions, music, even a visit to the Great Exhibition in Paris, sponsored by my firm. Designers then were expected to absorb the mood of the times so their work could catch the crest of the wave and be forward looking.

After my war service as a Paymaster in my own right and PA to the Captain – pay then involved welfare, as well as dealing with the money – the studio seemed too enclosed as a way of life. While I was considering going back, the Greek designer who was head of the studio died, and this decided me to go to Hornsey College of Art to take the Teacher's Diploma, on a WRNS

Officer's grant. This meant starving in a garret on £3 per week. Hornsey gave me an evening class to help. The Intermediate was a qualifying exam that had to be taken in two terms. There was no opportunity for me to choose another craft; it had to be silk weaving, as I already had Leeds University Diploma in Textile Industries, and had specialised in silk. Hand weaving as taught and practised then struck me as appalling.

As I had only a short time before the Intermediate Examination, I was filled with dismay when I saw most of the weaving that was being done at Hornsey. It looked to me very unenterprising, in fact really dull. However, a weaving friend, Marjorie, a little hunchbacked girl, because I was disappointed with some weaving, said, 'I know of an exciting weaver. One Saturday you must come down to Gospels at Ditchling and meet her, because I think you'd like what was there.'

With Marjorie I went down to Ditchling to see Ethel Mairet. We used to pay a guinea for this privilege, spend the day there, absorb the atmosphere, lunch at Maud Partridge's guest house down the road and pay a few extra shillings for scraps from the waste bag. These visits helped me to pass the weaving part of the Inter with flying colours, and I continued to make happy visits to Ditchling whenever possible.

Weavers will like to know that my exam project was to design and weave suitable curtains for a seaside bungalow. They had to be cheap and practical. Mine were in Gospels' yellow cotton space warp, a fancy yarn, four times as thick as the cotton used as an overcheck, with pull-up loops in this yarn to form centres in alternate squares. This caused an absolute furore at Hornsey. The weaving teacher took it to the head, Mr Moody, in her worried distress, and the word came back from on high that Mary Barker was to pull out these lumps and bumps at once, and even then she was probably doomed to failure. Now WRNS paymasters are not used to being told what to do. I have known them to query the Director of Navy Accounts himself, if they are confident of their figures. So I stuck to my guns, praying that Gospels' influence was to be trusted. It was. So I had more reason than ever to revere Ethel Mairet. Incidentally, when I began going to Gospels, I had been a little hurt by her apparent dislike of me.

Later on I found it was my Leeds and Art School training that met with her disapproval. She welcomed Marjorie with open arms, but I comforted myself that my friend got special attention as an ex-pupil and possibly because of her disability.

My health at this time was at a low ebb – I had always been subject to fainting. At morning prayers in school and in church services, there I might be falling flat, being a nuisance. To this day, I avoid going to church except for family weddings and funerals. I never actually fainted on parade – but that was probably because I was usually in command of the Wrens and could move around. As I grew older, if I felt faint, I could take precautions – breathe deeply or find fresh air – but often I would faint without warning. This tendency was inherited from my mother and my grandmother. Living for so many years with the navy, fatty cocoa and rancid fat to spread on bread, left me with gall bladder trouble. Living on a grant of £3 a week did not help. The local hospital X-rayed me and prescribed a strict diet. Rationing was in force. For a year stewed apple, baked beans and black tea or coffee were the main ingredients in my daily meals, together with any wholemeal bread and salad obtainable. The hospital kept an eye on me and I avoided the operation, but it put me off baked beans for the rest of my life.

Eventually I got my qualification of Artist Teaching Diploma. I still continued going down to Ditchling and it turned out that there were three facts of life that Ethel Mairet and I had in common. We both came from the West Country. She from Barnstaple, myself from Long Ashton, outside Bristol, and we loved the countryside dearly. We were both eldest daughters of scientific fathers and they had early taught us to have questioning minds. Then to crown it all, I got the teaching job at Brighton College of Art in 1950 that had once been hers. The cupboards there had been turned out, but otherwise it was much as she had left it. Hornsey and my background there were forgiven and she suggested that I came to Gospels for the week-end on the way to London and worked my passage. This meant that on finishing my Friday evening class at 9.30, I nipped across the road, just caught the last bus for Ditchling, toiled wearily down the Beacon Road to Gospels, where the front door was left unlatched for me, and tottered up to bed in the little room at the head of the stairs. At eight o'clock in the morning, she used to bang on the door and say, 'Your turn for the bathroom, and wake Doctor Collingwood when you've done.' I used to stagger down to the kitchen later for a mug of good hot coffee and home-made bread and honey, and then into the studio, where I was put to work.

Believe it or not, we were still on rations in 1950 and I brought my own. At first I was set to weave on whatever lengths of cloth needed finishing on the looms. These were for Ethel Mairet's shop in East Street and you had to continue from the last person's work. It was most important that you beat up the cloth the same as your predecessor – light beat for dress fabrics, a heavy one for coatings. It was not always easy to follow the last person exactly. Leeds University had taught me to count picks per inch, so I surreptitiously brought my piece glass with me. This was not enjoyable work and luckily Ethel soon decided she could find a better use for me and my experience. So I began to weave the 'one offs', cushions, bordered fabrics, stoles, scarves and, of course, I worked on the gauze looms. These latter were on the ground floor of the outside studio beyond the dye house, a bitterly cold place in winter. In fact a great many memories of Gospels are tinged with bitter cold. That somehow threw up in contrast the glowing richness of all the colours surrounding one in the studio. There was always an organised muddle of finished pieces, freshly dyed yarns hung up, the latest order in from Maygroves, the manufacturer who supplied cottons, and new samples from overseas to try.

The pattern of the Gospels working day was to start around 8.30 to 9.00 a.m. in the studio. The old stove, however, was already lit, and a variety of pots to be stirred often stood on top. Some of these were wool mordanting or dyeing, and often there was in addition the lunchtime stew. Around 10.30 to 11 there was a break for coffee. This earned me the nickname of 'Teacher's Pet' because if the sun was shining even in midwinter, Ethel would call me out to sit by the garden table in that sunny corner of the house, eat an apple and talk, usually garden and country things at that time of day.

In my time there were four large treadle looms on the ground floor. One was a large double countermarch Lervald make, with eight shafts if need be. This loom stood under the gallery. On the right-hand side, opposite, was a stout 'no name' simple four-shaft treadle loom, sturdy to weave coatings and other heavy weights. Peter Collingwood was weaving on this while I was there. Behind, on the left, was another loom, rarely used. Near the side entrance stood an elderly, very simple, four-shaft loom, that Ethel often used. It may have been the very loom that featured in the photo of herself at Norman Chapel. There the warping mill stood nearby with a heck-block on which she wound the warps, 30 yards long and with many ends in a portee. Upstairs in the gallery, under the window was a small scarf loom and against the window a rug loom that Dorothy Ablett used. I remember a book-case with the sample books stacked in the corner.

Dark corners had many cobwebs at this time, dust was fairly thick and one worried about the ravages of moths among textiles collected from all over the world. Among valuable sample lengths I remember enjoying best the beautiful Rodier cloths kept in the chest in the sitting room. It was always good to prowl round and have a look at what was being sent in to add to her collection. The charlady, Mrs Seymour, who travelled out from Brighton, did her best but was not allowed to tidy the studios. Nothing being used was to be moved. Mrs Seymour was always a good friend to me.

Downstairs, keeping out some of the draught from the main studio entrance, was a large screen, the cloth painted with the processes of weaving, which always intrigued me. There was also a large chest of drawers in which samples and records were kept. Among these I was particularly interested in the silks, often using Erie, a honey-coloured thick, native silk mixed with other threads, in self-colour and shadow-stripe chevrons made by S and Z contrast spun yarns.

The first warp I wove on was a fine red woollen on the Lervald. It was in plain weave, a black and an orangey-pink making small weft stripe effects. This type of fabric, often with pick and pick effects, with contrast in colour, was often woven in my day. I really thought something a little more exciting could have been done – however, they sold well at the East Street shop. The long warp of my first length had been deplorably wound on, and progress was halted with many ends to repair. We were expected to weave fairly fast – half a yard per hour – and match the last person's work so perfectly that no join showed. Fortunately the scarf and stole warps were shorter – perhaps 6 to 12 yards. At this time I was experimenting with grouped weaves, hand gauzing, and spacing both warp and weft, to produce light open structures. Ethel Mairet understood and appreciated this and she usually put fine black cotton or wool on the small loom so that I could do my experiments on this, just re-reeding the warp between stoles. There must have been another smaller loom in the main studio because I can recall weaving many an inlay cushion on a wide warp, sometimes with pull-up loops, sometimes cut ends making a fringe, sometimes just tufts.

Ethel Mairet, probably because it was not a thing that she herself was good at, disapproved strongly of any design made first on paper. I found this inhibiting and made tiny scribbles on the back of envelopes hidden in my handbag, to ensure that the balance was right. Only a thumbnail sketch was needed so that I could make sure that all proportions were correct in the design before starting to weave. People working in the studio were so in awe of her that one really had to resort to subterfuge on occasion.

There was a long shelf under the window leading to the little office from which one entered the main house, on which lived, in a jumbled order, many *objets trouvés;* enough inspiration there to gladden any art student's heart. All around were scattered yarns in glowing colours, madder and indigo, fighting with the brilliant yellows, blues and reds, chemically dyed rows of cottons and wools of every thickness. One rummaged around until the right colour and textile count came to hand. In the little office the heap system of filing held sway, but usually Ethel Mairet could put her hand on what she needed without delay.

Come 12.30-ish it was down to Maud Partridge's guest house for lunch. Maud was Ethel's sister. After this little boarding house was closed, I fed at various places in the village. Towards the end I was allowed to share the lunchtime stew. After lunch, if the day had warmed up, I went to the gauze looms in the outer studio.

Both the narrow and wide ones of these were warped with black and gold stripes, alien to my ideas because everything had a wasp-like look. They did not work as well as those I had used at Leeds. We went up wooden stairs from this studio to the upper floor, where there were piles of all sorts of exciting fibres and yarns, things like raffia and sea grass, and some exotic rayon staple which again was dyed in excessively brilliant colours by the manufacturer.

Ethel Mairet retired to rest after lunch until about 3 p.m. and one was not allowed to disturb her for any reason. At about two o'clock I came back into the main studio on Saturday to receive visitors, Sunday too. I did my best to keep them happy until three, but was not really a successful salesgirl. In this way I met numbers of interesting people from home and abroad. When she did come back down, Ethel Mairet sparkled with excitement when at last she realised who had come and was soon busy talking to them.

Soon after 5 p.m. we had our frugal, healthy supper at the scrubbed kitchen table – home-made bread, salad, perhaps some cooked vegetarian dish or soup then fruit, with Earl Grey tea – all in decorated multi-coloured pottery, a joy to look at. It was a silent meal but the best was to come. When Peter Collingwood was there, he would go out to visit friends in the village, but there was the wood fire in the sitting room to be lit and Ethel Mairet settled down to listen to the 6 p.m. news on the radio. When this was done she talked, talked really in capital letters. I spun, listening, on the little red wheel that Marion Boniface later found and rescued from a junk shop. At first I used to listen, but in the end I talked back.

Ethel Mairet had an alert, noticing mind, vigorous in defining her views, at first appearing intolerant, but responding to reasoning backed by fact. She respected knowledge, particularly of textile technique. Conversations would begin about politics and personalities in the news, then range over her travels, people she had met, things she had seen and done. She was interested in what I had seen since my last visit, what theatres, concerts, art exhibitions, and she always tried to understand why I so loved ballet, the art of movement. She spoke longingly of the West

Country that I often visited, asking for news of the house she had built at Saunton Sands. She loved all country pursuits. She once shouted at me to rush up to the gallery to watch the hounds, huntsmen in their pink coats and horses in all colours gallop by, partly across the garden. Eventually, our talks would come round to the new book she planned. Lewis Munford's book *Technique and Civilisation* was often quoted. Her book was to include further development of themes she had written about before, but particularly stressing the need for the relationship between science and craft to be understood.

She took a tremendous interest in what my young students were doing at Brighton College of Art and each year, I suppose 1950, 1951 and 1952, sometime in the summer term, they would come out to Gospels for a visit. She was very generous in answering their questions, but towards the end she would get tired of them and say to me, 'You answer that.' They thought it was absolutely splendid and revelled in exploring the different yarns. She would often give them small spools to try out and I think it generally woke up their ideas. In fact during her last year, I persuaded the twins Barbara and Gillian Batt to go out and weave for her, but of course she could not pay them very well and they soon left. Eventually both of them taught, Barbara very success-fully at the Gloucester School of Art.

The Head of the Dress and Textiles at Brighton, Mary Bryan, was very agitated one morning when I got down from London, wanting to know if I had confirmed that it was right for our visit to take place that day. I told her it was all fixed up, no need to panic. She said, 'I rang up and only got a reply from someone that she wasn't there.' I said I expected it would be all right but with such chivvying going on, I rang Ethel Mairet again during her lunchtime.

'Oh,' she said, 'what are you fussing for?'

I said, 'You know they rang from Brighton and heard you weren't there.'

It turned out that she had been into Brighton herself to have her hair done because students, who included quite a few young men, were coming out that afternoon. The visit happened; Mary Bryan nipped through the garden over the bridge to call on Charles Knight, later our Vice Principal, who lived in the adjoining house, and my students and I had our usual enjoyable exploring time.

Each week Ethel gave herself a day off, either morning or afternoon. She took a bus (and in those days there were many buses going through Ditchling) in a new direction. She said to me one day, 'You will enjoy being old, dear'. I looked a bit surprised. She explained, 'You can get on the bus and if you don't see any-one interesting on the lower deck, you climb upstairs, you look for the most interesting person to talk to and you sit down beside them.' I could not help laughing, but now I am even older than she was and can imagine doing much the same sort of thing.

A dressmaker who came in to collect the finished fabrics, which sometimes were made up before they went into her shop in East Street, Brighton, told me that Ethel had been a beauty. She described her going to some evening party, rather a Bohemian affair. She was dressed in a long, full, somewhat peasant-like dress with a vivid green shawl wrapped round her shoulders and in those days her hair was red.

I cannot really describe what she looked like because it was not her looks, it was the whole person, that I admired. I never even really noticed what she was wearing. She used to scold me and say, always, 'Anything to do with weaving, the Guilds, or anywhere you go to, you should wear something hand-woven.' I think East Sussex Guild must have noticed by now that I usually try to wear something of my own make at a meeting. She felt it helped. I was terribly distressed when she died but glad for her that it came so quickly. I went home to London on the Sunday, instead of staying over until Monday morning, because it promised to be a foggy night. I went into Brighton to lunch with a friend at the Old Ship Hotel, went back by the afternoon train and it was not until I got down to Brighton on the Wednesday that they rang up to say that Ethel had died on the Monday. When I got to the studio, after the funeral, I went to the loom on which she had been trying to tie up the harness. On her last Sunday morning she crawled from underneath and said simply, 'I feel old today, it's making me giddy. You'd better get under and tie it up.' I was so pleased to see that she had woven most of a length on that Sunday afternoon and Monday morning. I think she just went up to rest after lunch and must have died in her sleep. For several years I missed her and Ditchling very much indeed. I was not happy with the new regime and it was not until Tadek Beutlich came and rejuvenated it, giving it some lively atmosphere again, that I enjoyed going out there.

I did not know then that Ditchling was the home of my ancestors, and that, possibly, was why it was always a happy place for me. It was not until I took up family history research in the mid 1970s that I found out that George Wood was a farmer living at 7 East End Lane. He died in 1662, leaving his farm to his grandson, Harry Wood. The Wood Family was descended from Thomas Awoode and his wife Joan, who lived at Awoode's Place, later called Hammonds Place. There is a monument to Thomas in Clayton Church, dated 1508–9; he had bought the copyhold of Burgess Hill. My connection with this family comes from my great-grandmother, born Clara Ann Wood. I never knew her – although my great-grandfather lived until 1914 and I remember him well – but an enlarged photograph of Clara Ann smiles down on me as I write this. Friends say I look like her.

Ethel Mairet built Gospels in 1919, soon after the war, and, as she had done up in the Midlands, she ran Gospels as a weaving school. Students came both from England and overseas to join her workshop. The house itself was comfortable, although it had bare wooden floors, cottage-type doors and an Aga in the tiled kitchen. It was built on an L-shape, making that sunny corner where we had our 11 o'clock drink.

Her first husband's second wife had come one summer to write a joint biography. I was forbidden the place for a month, but had bulletins from neighbours and Mrs Seymour, the cleaning lady, that all was not going well. This lady left a case of Sanatogen Tonic Wine as a present. Ethel was not very sure that she would like this but I announced it was a good tonic. So from then on we used to have a glass of this wine with our mid morning apple, sitting in the sunshine, whenever it was possible. I liked the open fire that was built straight on the hearth in the living room. The kitchen seemed to me cold. Even the Aga there, which was supposed to make it the one warm room in the house, did not succeed in doing so. The scullery was pretty basic. Everything had been concentrated in the weaving rooms. It had been built for 30 years when I knew it from 1947 onwards, but it was from 1950–52 that I started staying there regularly.

Thirty years later, when Margot Coatts had done the research and published her book on Ethel Mairet, there was a conference about her in the Birmingham Museum, together with an exhibition. Marianne Straub, Margot herself and an architect were to lecture, Marianne as an ex-pupil and a great friend, was to speak about life and work at Gospels, Margot would describe Ethel's life and the architect would describe Norman Chapel, the historic house where she had lived for a while with her first husband, Ananda Coomaraswamy. Unfortunately Marianne had a heart attack in Switzerland so I went as a substitute.

Rereading *A Weaver's Life – Ethel Mairet 1872-1952* has brought back my Ditchling days spent at Gospels vividly to mind. But even the book's superb photography, by David Cripps, of Ethel Mairet's weaving cannot reproduce the blaze of colour warming the icy-cold weaving studio. You need to handle the work to appreciate the quality and variety of the yarns used – while your eye feasts on the madder reds, the weld yellows and the indigo blues. The white and black rugs and stoles, the subtle neutrals often in silk and linen acted as a contrast to make more vivid those primary colours.

Thirty years was a long time and I could not help chanting to myself, 'Too little and too late', because textiles do not last for ever. They have been scattered, and some of the best ones had been sold. The exhibition was fairly representative but it did not really give that glorious feast of colour that I had known in the untidy studios at Gospels itself. However, when the exhibition was moved to London they included furniture, like the dining table and one or two other things from Gospels. Mr Southern had lived there with his wife after their return from Africa and had changed the atmosphere. They had brought back no end of native textiles. The place was scrubbed and thoroughly cleaned and somehow did not feel or look quite right. Then Tadek Beutlich came and brought renewed life. He did his tremendous sisal free wall hangings; they were elemental, sometimes in neutrals and sometimes very colourful, and it did bring back creative life that Ethel would have enjoyed. Eventually he moved to Spain. The property was bought by four men; three were at the Mairet Exhibition when it came to the Craft Centre in London and they met me. They said, 'Do come and have a look at the place and see if you think Ethel Mairet would have approved of what we have done to it.' I felt that Dorothy Ablett ought to come with me, because she was a Ditchling girl.

The Sunday arranged was unfortunately the Sunday after the Grand Hotel was bombed at the Conservative Conference. However, we went and they put me in one of the chairs that had been left behind, one of the chairs she was very fond of, sitting her side of the fire. They had left the hearth – it was pretty much the same as it had been before, except for some very elegant fire-dogs. They took me into the weaving studio, which now had been cleaned and redecorated beautifully. All the wood was polished and there was a long refectory dining table there with chairs around. There was a candelabra, and in the gallery they had draperies or oriental rugs hanging over the rail. I am sure Ethel would have enjoyed seeing it in that state. The kitchen had been completely modernised too. They had enclosed the yard which was used for dyeing, between the house and the garden studio, and this was now their summer dining room. They had green plants and palms and white garden furniture round the table in there, all very elegant. Upstairs there had been renovation; more bathrooms put in and two more bedrooms made from the upstairs studio. All in all, I felt that although it was changed, it was altered in a way that she would have enjoyed.

7

The Weavers Journal

The January sun was shining gaily on the pile of yarns in brilliant reds, yellows, blues, greens – every colour imaginable. These were lying on the desk of the Head of Women's Crafts, Sheila MacEwan, at Hornsey College of Art. I was just going when she called me back. 'Mary, the Guilds are bringing out a journal and I would like you to be Secretary. I am going to be Chairman of the Editorial Committee, and Elsie Davenport is on the Committee.' So without thinking any more seriously about it, I just said casually, 'Yes, certainly.' Thus I landed myself with a problem child that would last me for more than 30 years.

Sheila had been very kind to me when, in 1947, I first went back to Hornsey School of Art on a WRNS officer's grant of £150 pounds per year to get an Art Teacher's Diploma. She gave me an evening class in weaving to help my finances. Now by 1952 my work had built up so that I was teaching at Hornsey for two whole days per week, morning, noon and evening, as well as two and a half days at Brighton. Sheila went on to tell me that it would not involve much work being Secretary. She added that Mrs Broadbent, an elderly teacher who used to take the Pedagogy Class at Hornsey, was going to be Treasurer. My consenting to do the job of Secretary without thinking more deeply about it was because of my gratitude to Sheila. London Guild had been launched two or three years previously and by now she was Chairman. My friend Enid Russ (who had learnt weaving from me, as well as Sheila) and I had joined London as founder members, so we knew about the Guild movement. Elsie

Davenport, ex-Hornsey, then a well-known freelance hand weaver, was also involved, both with the Guild and the *Journal*. This meant that there were four of us on the *Journal* Committee from Hornsey College of Art and this really set the attitude and approach. Quality of work and design was a fundamental principle for all the time that I was connected with the *Journal*. I always wanted a Committee Member to be a current teacher in an art college so that we could see these standards were not only maintained but kept up to date. The other members of the *Journal* Committee were Hilary Bourne, Alice Hindson, Mr F. Dickinson and Hester Viney.

Hilary, then, was a well-known freelance weaver. She is now the Curator of the Ditchling Museum. Alice Hindson was known for draw loom weaving, in which she specialised. Hester Viney was Secretary of the Dorset Guild, one of the first to form after the 1939–45 war. Before the war she had been concerned with the early Guild of Weavers, Spinners and Dyers, which unfortunately had not survived. She was instrumental in encouraging counties to form their own Guilds and had, with Somerset, a hand in arranging the Meeting of Guilds in November 1951.

Ethel Mairet, when she had heard of this journal, did consent to write a not very enthusiastic word of welcome for it, which was duly published in Number 1. She said to me, 'You know, I don't think you are very wise to entangle yourself with that thing. It will take too much of your time. You still have your way to make, and you enjoy teaching and you will eventually have a full-time job.' I fear I did not take too much notice of her warning because I had already become a member of the Craft Centre of Great Britain, which was then centred in Hay Hill, just off Bond Street in London. They usually managed to sell anything I had time to weave. I was a Fellow of the Arts and Crafts Exhibition Society (later the Society of Designer Craftsmen) so I felt I was on the road to being a recognised craftsman. Surely I'd have time to do a few letters! As I enjoyed weaving and was fairly fast and my stoles were selling well, it seemed I was lucky. The Arts and Crafts Exhibition Society sent an exhibition to Milan. I submitted four silk scarves and sold three of them. Perhaps I needn't take too much notice of her warning. I thought. What foresight she had. For the next 31 years much of my spare time was spent in the *Journal's* service. Looking back it is impossible to decide whether it was a worthwhile task or not. But for the first decade continuity was needed to ensure survival.

I sometimes now wonder what my life would have been if I had recognised that besides her wonderful creative ability Ethel Mairet still had a fund of wisdom and was very shrewd about prospects. Anyway, the die was cast, and she did not live to see the result. The first few meetings of the *Journal* Committee didn't cause me much trouble. Correspondence was beginning to be much more of a headache when, suddenly, in 1953, after a year in office, both Sheila MacEwan and Elsie Davenport resigned from the Committee. Hilary Bourne took over as Chairman. I felt quite unthreatened by extra work for a meeting or two, but Hilary also had a career as a hand loom weaver to follow. This was not buttressed by teaching at two art schools. So the workload became more and more my responsibility. Now those war years had made a tremendous impression on me. When you were pointed towards anything, you had to carry on and do it, it was your duty, and I was beginning to be fond of the *Journal*, and believed it would help to raise the standard of weaving and the associated crafts throughout the whole country (still in my mind, pretty low), so I persevered. With hindsight, perhaps, it was not such a bad idea because the *Journal* brought me a tremendous number of friends, and pleasure as well as anxiety and pain. It was through the *Journal* that I got my two lovely overseas tours to Australia and New Zealand. Eventually I travelled across North America as well. Keeping the *Journal* afloat proved to have been a more rewarding task than my teaching, which, after all, was my paid job.

Soon after Sheila had asked me to be Secretary, the first Editorial Committee meeting was held. We met at the flat of our Editor, Joanna Bourne, who was a sub-editor of *Time and Tide*. She had a flat over the offices in one of those tall period houses in Bloomsbury not far from the British Museum. Sheila produced an agenda, typewritten at Hornsey for this meeting, introduced me as Secretary and it was agreed that I was not to have a vote. I cannot remember then if the Honourable Treasurer was allowed one. It was quite amusing not to be allowed a vote, because with my Textile Diploma from Leeds University Textile Department, my knowledge of fibres and all their processes was probably more thorough and deeper than any of the others'. However, in 1952 most hand weavers despised industrial weaving and did not credit it with the skill and knowledge that it undoubtedly had. Taking minutes was a nightmare, because it did not seem, although there was an agenda, to be anything more than a gathering of friends and as quite a few of them had definite bees in their bonnets about subjects they wished to promote, I began to wonder if we would ever see a journal at the end of the evening. We did not meet until 7.00 or 7.30 and we were supposed to end about 9.30. There was nothing formal, nothing ever came to a vote and my minutes became more like a little essay on the themes discussed. After the first few meetings there was never really time for me to read the minutes. They needed a secretary to run everything that happened in the three months between meetings. I became very overburdened and worried with the correspondence, some of which could not be answered off my own bat. Sheila was a tremendous back-up and help to me, but in our busy lives there was not much time and I often had to invent an answer – whatever might meet the occasion.

Mr Dickinson, the Advertisement Manager, was a great stand-by. I could get him on the telephone and if there was anything really worrying about production or business, he could always advise me on what to say. I think he had been elected onto the Committee because he was a well-known weaver, Gladys Dickinson of Somerset's brother. He certainly was very able in getting the advertisements which provided us with some revenue.

For many years the *Journal* was printed by the Ditchling Press. Both Hilary and Joanna Bourne came from Ditchling and knew the printer there. We had very good service from Ditchling, but the trouble was that we were such a small order to begin with. We were unprofessional in that we did not keep to times and dead-lines so that the *Journal* often came out late.

We worked absolutely on a shoestring. The ten Guilds, Founder Guilds who were very proud of having started this, were Cornwall, Devonshire, Dorset, Gloucestershire, Hallamshire and

District, Hampshire, London and Home Counties, Kent, Warwickshire with Worcestershire and Staffordshire and Somerset. The reserve working fund was given by members of the Founder Guilds, and in an old notebook I found that it was £153 1s 10d. Each of them gave what they could afford. There is a mention of donations which amounted to £21 9s 6d and much, much later when the old pre-war National Guild was wound up, the *Journal* was presented with the sum of £89 0s 10d. It was not a very large working capital. The first issue, Number 1, March 1952, has on its cover 'Price 1/6 per copy; to Guild Members 1/'. This decision, which was made well before I came on the scene, has always been the cause of great worry to me. The sensible thing would have been, in the beginning, for Guilds to have included the price of the *Journal* in their Guild subscription, so that all members took the *Journal*. We could then have charged, as we always did, a little bit extra to the outside world. I can understand why this happened. The Guilds were all in operation, those ten, and one other that was very indignant at not being asked to the christening, namely my own Guild, Sussex – of that more later. Guild subscriptions varied between 5s and 10s a year. Most Guilds felt that it was unfair to add on the price of the *Journal*. They also raised the fact that one household with two members would pay for two *Journals* when they only needed one. Pre-war, there had been one countrywide Guild and at first one news-sheet, at which time the Journal was included in the subscription. Unfortunately the ten Guilds' wrong decision did mean that individual members had a choice as to whether they took the *Journal*. The situation has worsened so much that I am now very distressed when at meetings of Sussex Guild there is only a small heap of *Journals* waiting to be collected by members, when we are a Guild of over 200 strong. Only a tenth of our members still subscribe.

I once accused the *Journal* of becoming *Home Chat* in a *Vogue* cover. Since then it has had a new Editor and Printer. The typography and layout have changed to a more commercial image, less of an art format. If the policy about contributors does not become more outward looking, it will end up as an 'in-house' magazine. Most Guilds now run splendid newsletters with articles of their own, so *Journal* sales will decline still further. Members subscribe to overseas textile magazines in search of inspiration. Once upon a time, young artist craftsmen were pleased to have their work illustrated in the *Journal*. It brought new ideas to guild weavers and in return gave a certain amount of publicity to the craftsmen as our non-guild subscribers included museums, art galleries, colleges of art and other education establishments both at home and overseas.

To return to the scene of that first Editorial Committee meeting. It was held in a small room round an oblong table, in poor light. We had climbed a lot of stairs to get there. My position was just a little to the rear of Sheila MacEwan, the Chairman, so that she could give me a helping hand with the minutes. She was a good Chairman, businesslike and direct, but even at that early stage people wanted to air their views. There was not enough time for them all to have a full say. They concentrated mostly on what they found wrong with the last *Journal*. For many, many years, I tried to make them explain the fault briefly and firmly. In our two-hour meeting the chief preoccupation should have been getting out the next copy. Elsie Davenport had been through the articles, making amendments and corrections. Journal Number 1 was by this time already in the hands of the printer, so everyone was in full cry. I found it was almost impossible to take minutes as there was so much of what, to me, were rather unnecessary elaboration of theories, ideas and so forth. Very interesting, but there was Number 2 to consider. Hilary Bourne, with her charming warmth and welcome, feeling much at home with her sister there as Editor, set a pattern of informality and one realised how valuable it was. In all my days I tried to keep the same atmosphere, but also to be firm about the passage of time.

One practical note about the first meeting was that Mr Dickinson reported that he had 11 advertisements for the next issue, Number 2, and there were also seven 'smalls' from private members and a Guild, to put in. In the editorial for Issue Number 2, the Editor says, 'We find that this issue, to our surprise, and gratification has nearly paid for itself; but nearly is not quite, and our aim is to be completely self-supporting by the end of year.' That must have been the hope of every editorial committee right up to the present day. Our fortunes have had rather a peculiar temperature chart and Alice Hindson later gave me a list of the first ten years, showing how our fortunes rose and then dipped. As soon as the first issue came out, the flood of correspondence began. I think everyone was rather surprised how much there was. Unfortunately it was not really very helpful for the *Journal*. I had to answer a lot of personal queries. They did not really give us any help about what weavers did want in the *Journal* – where can I buy so and so? How can I learn to weave? What is so and so? Where do I sell my work?

About this time a firm had set up making looms – Weavemaster; not, to my mind, good looms, but with them came a very simple little brochure telling people how to set them up, and they advertised with slogans like 'Buy a loom and earn your living'. Of course, it was very difficult for any but the best artist-craftsmen, and weavers, to find a market for their work. There was then the Red Rose Guild, which had an exhibition annually in Manchester, which sold work. I had been fortunate there and as well as at the Craft Centre of Great Britain in Hay Hill, but to be a member, you had to belong to one of five Art Societies. In 1950 I had been accepted by what is now the Society of Designer Craftsmen, then the Arts and Crafts Exhibition Society, for my weaving. Guild members had their own Guild Annual Exhibitions where they sold their work but that did not reach a very large market. Many artist-craftsmen had other outlets for their work. Heals (a London furniture store) helped. They were then showing a certain amount of hand-made rugs and hangings, and later, people began to develop private clients by recommendation. Occasionally collectors or buyers came over from Europe or America, and through the Craft Centre, I had an offer to buy my hand-woven stoles from one of the big firms in America. However, they wanted something like a hundred a quarter, and when you think of my very full-time programme of teaching between Hornsey and Brighton I simply could not manage numbers like that. Several of the pitiful letters from weavers hoping to find markets for their work were shown to Sheila MacEwan and Elsie Davenport and perhaps this led to their resigning from the *Journal* Committee at the end of the first year.

Another frequent subject was 'Why aren't we on the cover? We were in existence,' said Sussex, 'when those ten Guilds met.' And they felt that there was some privileged society to which they could not belong. Each time those original ten Guilds met and had a discussion, they called themselves the Council of Representatives of the Guild. Their acting Honourable Secretary, Dorothy Luke, later wrote a very good article explaining how the Guilds began the *Journal*, but this was not much comfort to Sussex and the other outside Guilds. Even in the summer of 1952, she and I had been so worried by letters from Guild Secretaries who were not among the chosen ten, that we began to think that there should be some sort of Association or Federation. From my point of view it was essential that all Guilds subscribed to the *Journal* and I felt that they needed to feel part of it.

Those Annual Meetings of the Council of Representatives were an ordeal, because it was my task to present the Editorial Committee's report on the year. It was a case of listening to all the complaints about lateness; how somebody did not like such and such an article; and why couldn't we do so and so; whereas I very often did not even have the support of the Treasurer and had to point out our financial situation. They often behaved as if we had the resources of *The Times* or other national newspapers at our disposal. Anyone who has a copy of Number 9, the March 1954 *Journal*, can read all about association in Miss Luke's article. In 1953, after 18 Guilds were sent circulars and a copy was also printed in the following issue of the *Journal*, replies were received from 14 and were read at the meeting. Of these, seven approved the idea with reservations, mainly concerned with the expense involved, limitation of freedom etc. Four were uncertain, feeling that the time was not yet ripe. Three definitely declined to be considered in connection with the matter. This, broadly speaking, was an even balance of for and against and left the matter where it started.

I am now going to quote from a good article by Hester Viney, where she speaks of the advantage of federation or association. Her article is called 'The Foundation and Development of The Country Guilds'. It appeared in *Journal* Number 5 in March 1953. She spoke then about a federation or an association or a council of all Guilds which could best serve their needs – these are some of them:

A combined exhibition of the work of all the Guilds, a central library service and information bureau, a travel service to see work on the Continent and overseas, a list of lecturers and teachers at approved fees, a travelling exhibition of fine weaving samples, etc.

It is good, now, to realise how the Association of Guilds has coped with all of these. We now have a National Exhibition every second year, a splendid Summer School in the alternate years. We have not got a central library service but there is a book list. An approved list of lecturers and teachers is kept, for which Guilds can write. The travel service to see work on the Continent and overseas has been run by individuals, not necessarily by the Guilds. This has been a success and usually each year there is something advertised in the *Journal* about a foreign tour. We do also advertise workshops regularly. I always felt that if we could have had a travelling exhibition of fine weaving samples in the early days, it would have been a tremendous help to newcomer Guilds about standards of quality in both workmanship and design. Early in my teaching, from 1950 onwards, the Victoria and Albert Museum sent round a collection of textiles to art schools. It was a great help to my students to see these.

Two factors kept the need for some sort of federation to the forefront of my mind. One was that Sussex Guild, in existence when the Guilds first met to plan the *Journal*, kept harping on about not being invited. The other was that my secretarial experience had been under King's Regulations and Admiralty Instructions, where there was a pattern for everything. With no definite organisation – no boss, in fact, to appeal to – in times of crisis everything was left on the Secretary's plate. Meetings only occurring once every three months meant that in urgent matters a phone call could be made to one or two people, who then talked rather expensively at long distance. They usually did not produce any very practical suggestions. Something had to be done – and I had to decide on my own.

During the period before the Association we were threatened with a lawsuit. It happened like this. Someone had brought a yarn remainder from one of our advertisers and had been commissioned to weave an altar frontal for a church, a commemorative piece. She had used this remainder yarn, yarn which unfortunately was not colour fast, so when it faded, on being kept on view in the church, they complained to her and she wrote to the *Journal*. It had been an expensive commission. It seemed that some legal action could be threatened. We simply had not the finances to deal with all this. As always, until his sudden death in January 1956, Mr Dickinson was approached for his practical knowledge and sturdy common sense and he gave me the answers to write. In this case, he said he would ask a legal friend but our advertiser's products were not our responsibility and all that was necessary was to write a letter of commiseration.

The second meeting of the Guilds' Council of Representatives had already started talking about forming a loose Association of Guilds to be considered by every Guild and asking for suggestions and opinions. Sheila MacEwan had apologised for the absence of the Secretary and the Treasurer at this Council Meeting, held in Taunton on Wednesday 8 October 1952. She had also said that although we had got funds to cover the December issue without drawing on the sinking fund, our Editor, who was a professional journalist, regarded this as quite good and felt that we would pay our way during the next year.

As I have said, our first year ended with a bombshell when Sheila and Elsie announced their intention of resigning immediately from the *Journal* Committee. Sheila also resigned from being Chairman of the London Guild. This was a great blow to us because Elsie had collected the articles and supervised them. In a way her decision was understandable because she was very busy with three books, *Your Handweaving, Your Yarn Spinning* and *Your Yarn Dyeing*. Both she and Sheila felt that they were giving up all their spare time to weaving and these projects.

Hilary Bourne took over as Chairman of the Editorial Committee and Hilda Breed, who was then a lecturer in textiles at Avery Hill Training College, took over the collection and correction of articles. Hilda continued to do this for many, many years. She was excellent at cutting out passages from too verbose articles and knitting them together in the same sort of language that the author had used. I never had any complaints from those authors that they had been cut short or altered in any way – this was a great gift. The only worry about Hilda's long service was that, particularly after she retired, she got her papers in a muddle, even leaving some articles behind, thus delaying the meeting. She always felt that we should have more time for meetings, but that was the view of a retired person. We all of us had our jobs and this was the only time that most of us could spare. The other vacancy on the Committee was taken by John Valentine Kilbride, the well-known ecclesiastical weaver, with his workshops at the St Dominic's Guild, Ditchling Common.

By December 1954, Peter Collingwood, a freelance weaver with a workshop in North London, weaving mainly rugs on a many-shafted loom, had been co-opted on to the *Journal* Committee. Peter had been working at Gospels with Ethel Mairet when I first began weaving there at weekends and I already admired the clear, direct way he wrote articles on weaving. He reviewed the books which publishers sent us for the next 30-odd years.

This was before his book on rug weaving was published, but soon he began his workshop lecture tours to the United States, and indeed round the world, and these helped to publicise our *Journal*. He was very generous, writing articles until the early 1980s, when Victor Edwards, Chairman of the Association for some years, at last achieved his ambition of making the running of the *Journal* more democratic.

After Hilary had left for Yorkshire, we had to find a new Editor and also another place for the Committee to meet. Funds were still low and strict economy was needed. This ensured we had a small Committee. For a time Peter Collingwood was Chairman and we met at his mother's house. After Miss Good became Editor, her flat in St John's Wood was our meeting place. There was a time that we went to Gerald Crocker near Baker Street Station. Eventually Pat Tindale, an architect who had designed her delightful house just off Clapham Common, entertained us for several years. Pat was our Treasurer, so she understood the need for economy. Before meetings we had the extra interest of seeing what work was on her loom. It was here in 1983 that Kenneth Duncan broke the news that the original long-serving Committee was to be disbanded. Future members would be elected by the Association of Guilds at their Annual General Meeting, and nominated by the Guilds at regular intervals so that no one served more than three years, once the existing members had retired in rotation according to length of service. In some ways this was a good move to bring in a regular current of new ideas, but the *Journal* would not have survived its early years without a good measure of continuity. Sadly this manoeuvre meant that the up-and-coming young craftsmen would no longer have their work illustrated and reviewed in the *Journal*; it now looked to the Guilds for its material.

In the old days when Hilda Breed's cupboard was bare, we all had to turn to without delay and hastily write articles to fill up the *Journal*. These often turned out to be winners. As with theatres and plays, it was almost impossible to foresee which number would be a success. For years Alice kept a chart of our quarterly print order and the remainders for each number. Sometimes there would be few left, and we were left with the puzzle why that particular issue had been so successful.

In times of trouble, it was better that everyone looked outward for new material rather than inward at what Guilds were doing. This may be the secret of low circulation among some of the Guilds today. The Guilds know what their fellows do; they want to hear about what is being done in the world outside. This explains why other overseas magazines are ordered by the Sussex Guild in larger quantities than our own *Journal*.

Two patterns were developing. The first one was in the duties of the Committee. It really was more like a business now, with people in charge of different departments. This saved time. They could ring me if there was any query but for the three months between meetings they looked after their own patch unless a serious problem arose. Another pattern was in the contents. The regular features were editorial, the Guild reports (there was only room for three or four short ones per issue), forthcoming exhibitions and the advertisements which provided us with a good part of our income. We tried to include something of interest for more advanced weavers and a simple project for beginners. Then there was a general article, either some historic textile or ethnic weaving. Lastly, but very important, were the reviews of exhibitions. The editorial was always written by one of us because our Editor was not a weaver. In fact, this meant that we had to label diagrams and photographs so that we should get them into the *Journal* the right way up. Someone had to look after the non-Guild subscribers who were growing in number, and as they paid a more realistic price this was very necessary. Several libraries and colleges of art began to subscribe.

At this time a very general criticism from the Guilds was that most of the Committee were either London based or came from not too far away. This was a deliberate decision because of economising on train fares and phone bills. We were still very short of cash. It did not seem to matter whether the Committee Members belonged to the Guilds or not. We chose people at the beginning of their career, but with ideas so that we should not be stuck in a rut of tradition and historic weaving. Ann Whitehead (Bristow) was one of my early choices. She took over the non-Guild members and looked after the spare back numbers in her little house in Chelsea. When she eventually handed her job over to Gerald Crocker, it was an amusing occasion.

Ann was going to move away from London to a house in the country. She had a young baby to look after, so it was arranged that Gerald and I were to go to lunch with her to collect our property. The back numbers of the *Journals* and most of the correspondence concerning the non-Guild people were housed in her garage, which was two or three streets away. Ann drove Gerald round to the garage in her car and I had to follow, pushing the baby in the pram through the streets. I had not wheeled a pram for a great many years and Ann's baby did not know me very well, but she behaved admirably. By the time we got back to lunch, the baby was used to us and wanted to be one of the party. So during lunch Gerald nursed her and she generally stole the scene.

Gerald was a great acquisition. We started meeting at his flat, which was near Baker Street Tube Station. He became a great friend, not only of all Committee Members, but of his large parish of overseas subscribers. He was now retired and it became a hobby answering their letters. He made not only pen friends, but foreign weavers visited him when they came to London. I think it gave him a happy retirement in his old age.

Our sadness over his sudden death in May 1969 was compounded by the worry caused by the loss of all records, addresses and payments of the overseas non-Guild subscribers. I could never believe that as a retired bank official, he did not keep a neat record in some ledger. All we recovered from his relatives were letters and some scrappy notes in an envelope. Imagine the difficulties and delays in tracing our overseas subscribers. Fortunately Ruth Hurle added the overseas non-Guild subscribers to her non-members for Great Britain and Ireland. It is difficult for me to see those 31 years I spent as sheet anchor to the *Quarterly Journal* in perspective. Perhaps a look at what was happening in the larger textile field will give some framework to memory.

The end of the war had left the country with much to do. There was still rationing of food and clothing into the 1950s. Peacetime industries had to start up again. Demobilisation and closure of wartime factory production meant realignment of employment. Research for implements of war could now be directed to domestic production. The changeover took time because everyone was tired and had very little money. With great effort and government sponsorship, an exhibition of industrial goods was mounted.

In 1961 the Victoria and Albert Museum hosted an American Wall Hanging Exhibition in the small gallery adjoining the restaurant. Weavers here had already been experimenting in this medium for some years and were highly indignant that American examples had been shown first. So a committee – mostly *Quarterly Journal* personnel and friends – was formed to persuade the Victoria and Albert to put on a travelling exhibition for the British Wall Hangings. The museum selected Peter Collingwood's *Macrogauze* for the programme cover and my *Vision Blind* for the poster. For about a day I imagined my design posted up in every tube station, as was the museum's habit.

Disillusionment set in when the Prime Minister, Harold Wilson, announced an economy campaign, so 'my' poster just had a limited circulation to museums and galleries. I have never forgiven him!

Our wall hanging exhibition in 1965 was a great success although some Guild visitors complained of dust traps and silly useless objects. Most exhibits showed great technical skill as well as many original ideas that have inspired later developments. Peter Glen, the museum official who supervised selection and hanging of 'Weaving for Walls', wrote an article, both descriptive and analytical, for *Journal* Number 56, December 1965 that is interesting reading today.

Writing this 30 years later brings some of the exhibits vividly mirrored in memory: Tadek Beutlich's *Moon*, circular, transparent, with honesty seeds held between X-ray film, charred wood chips on a fragile open warp, unusual and unexpected material with which to create pure poetry; Theo Moorman's 3-D twisted constructions, contrasting with Ann Sutton's amusing use of yellow and orange double cloth pockets enclosing wood blocks alternating with perspex tubes. Another hint of sculpture infiltrating textile forms was Win Evans' *Nebula*; basically a red warp crossed with similar orange yarns on a copper wire to form the ground, inch-wide strips of aluminium were used as weft, stretching from selvedge to selvedge. These were bent up in a group at right angles and slope to the background, giving a 3-D effect, dazzling to the eye as different moving reflections were picked up. Joyce Griffiths showed her fragile, lacy, linen hangings enclosing skeleton leaves. Peter Collingwood showed *Macrogauze I*, the first of his crossed warp structures which later he developed into enormous 3-D structures.

The museum seemed pleased with this exhibition and most hangings travelled around the country, visiting Birmingham, Walsall, Wakefield, Birkenhead, Warwick, Glasgow, Barnsley, Huddersfield, Bethnal Green, Cardiff, Leamington, Reading and Kettering. Wouldn't young textile artists today be overjoyed if the Craft Council could organise a similar project for them.

In summer 1968, the Association of Guilds put on an

exhibition of furnishing materials for use in home and boardroom at the Building Centre, Store Street, London, WC1. Guilds had two categories of weavings at the Geffrye Museum, Kingsland Road, London, E3. In those days the young artist-craftsmen were glad to lend descriptions and photographs of their work to the *Quarterly Journal* and many told me how our overseas subscribers spread the word and helped with invitations to exhibitions and teaching tours. My own turn to travel was to come in 1970.

Edinburgh was as active in displaying fine textiles as London. The Scottish Craft Centre was a venue many weavers used to display work for sale. Above all there was the Dovecot Studio, where superb tapestry commissions were carried out, first from 1955 under the direction of Sax Shaw, and from 1960 by Archie Brennan and his team of artists. His own tapestries made a witty comment on contemporary lifestyle; his originality inspired others. The Scottish Arts Council had an exhibition of hand-woven and constructed hangings during the Edinburgh Festival, 15 August to 13 September 1970. Forty-four weavers contributed one work each. Entitled 'Modern British Hangings', the exhibition toured museums at Doncaster, Glasgow, Perth, Aberdeen, Manchester and Belfast.

Meetings from 1952 onwards seemed to be happy gatherings of friends. Little did they know that in the background they were being willingly subsidised by the heads of two departments in art schools in which I worked. Sheila MacEwan was always a tower of strength. I think she was sad that she had not stayed with the *Journal* and she was always there to help solve my problems for me. She allowed me to use the telephone in her office when I was teaching on my Hornsey days. Mary Bryan did the same for me at Brighton. Mary was not as enthusiastic about the aims of the *Journal* as Sheila, but she somehow regarded it as a feather in her own cap, because in those days both she and I were not only Fellows of the Arts and Crafts Exhibition Society (which later became the Society of Designer Craftsmen) but for a time we were both on the Council. She supposed that the *Journal* had something to do with that. I do not think this was the case; they regarded the Weavers' Guilds as not the same sort of craft that they were interested in. The Council was there to help the artist-craftsmen of the day find their exhibitions and their markets.

This happy arrangement of help lasted at Hornsey until I left for a full-time job at Brighton in 1959 and was still going on at Brighton when I packed up in summer 1970 to go on a lecture/workshop tour Down Under.

I had tried twice to leave the *Journal*, once in 1959 when I went down to Brighton on the full-time job. Living down there, I would not be on the spot for meetings. By then, I was acting as Chairman and it did not seem to me possible that it could run from Brighton. A London address would still be best. This, however, lasted no time at all. I stopped being involved with all the correspondence, but as of yore most problems still came to me.

Again, my overseas tour, the first one, was scheduled to last nearly a year. I did not resign from the Committee because I still wrote and sent them articles, but I definitely dropped out of 'office' and Win Evans took over from me as Chair. When I came back, New Zealand was already planning another lecture tour for me, on a grant this time. But I went to *Journal* meetings and generally took an interest. However, on my return from that second trip, which lasted only nine months, Win was already thinking that she had had enough, so for a time I acted as a runabout because I still had a pad in London. As I was retired I had time to go to exhibitions, to go and interview people, to collect information, so when Win finally went I just went back as Chairman, until eventually Kenneth Duncan replaced me.

8

Outside Events

When I was a child, it was a wonder how news was spread round the country. There was no radio or TV and we didn't have a telephone until we had been in the new house for some time; then our telephone number was Long Ashton 12. Father did take *The Times* each day but nobody else seemed to read it. It sat on a special corner of the billiard table until there was a top-heavy heap and then somebody took them up to a cupboard in the spare room. Later on I had ambitions of being a fashion artist and used to rummage among the old *Times* to search for drawings by Bessie Ascough, who was their fashion artist. No one seemed to notice the newspapers being disturbed. I never achieved that ambition but to this day, on the eve of my ninetieth birthday, I am still interested in dress.

The suffragette movement was going strong when I was a toddler. There was always plenty of gossip at tea parties about the movement. My mother, who was very lively and flirtatious, had no use for any village lady who hankered after the vote. 'Stuff and nonsense,' she would mutter on the way home. 'I have always got my own way, and so have all other women with any sense.'

The 1914–18 War put a damper on the suffragettes. Girls went into factories working on munitions, they became land girls and tried to do other work usually done by men, even joining the forces, with certain restrictions. I cannot even remember the date women got the vote, and there are only a tiny minority of women in Parliament today. True, we had a woman Prime Minister for quite a few years, but it was felt that one of the reasons why she was deposed was that her Cabinet began to feel irritated by being bossed about by a woman.

Wars like World War I and II bring about great changes in ordinary life whether a nation has been a winner or a loser. After the celebrations of the winners, or the despair of the defeated, both sides have to get back somehow to normal life. The difficulty here is that where men have been away from home fighting, risking their lives, they tend to return home expecting somehow to get back to the pattern of daily life they left when they joined up. But that routine has changed for ever. After the welcome by the family, they notice the difference, food rationing, parents have aged, wives have become self-sufficient running the home, babies have grown into older children, some rather irritated by having Father home and taking Mother's attention away from them. Even if their pre-war job has been held for them, that, too, will have changed. Industry no longer had to work full out producing everything needed for war. I suspect 'peace after war' is and has been a difficult time throughout history – how much does human nature change?

At some date in the 1930s, I worked for a man who had been called up in the Great War (as World War I was then called) aged 18, and after a short training, was sent out to France. Being an artist, he could describe his experiences so vividly that I could seem to see and hear them too. After a short spell at a training camp, their unit was sent to France. Travel was difficult, delays and then rushed journeys in dilapidated lorries. Eventually they made it to a rest camp a few miles behind the lines. They slept in tents, but there were a few tin sheds for mess and cooking. They were allowed a bucket of water per day for washing themselves and their clothes. They did a little drill, cleaned their rifles and their boots, played football and wrote letters home. Occasionally there were a few explosions in the neighbourhood and the odd aeroplane flew over. It was difficult to see its markings. They had got used to this easy life when word came through that they were to go up the line to replace a unit that had had bad casualties.

At first they marched along a dilapidated road on a sunny morning. A few strange gaunt trees still stood in a landscape once gentle hills, fertile fields and farms, but now devastated by shell holes and other debris. Birds were flying around singing as they tried to build their nests. This sight, the sunny morning, the rhythm of the march, had a calming effect for a time, but their march became interrupted as they had to climb into the ditch to leave room for a convoy of muddy trucks laden with wounded men, roughly bandaged, occasionally groaning at the inevitable jolts along the rutted road. The convoy passed slowly and was followed by the walking wounded. The landscape deteriorated. Some of the wounded had collapsed and were lying semi-conscious or dead alongside the road. The old hands were encouraging, chatting to cheer the rookies, but my friend, an artist, said his heart was sinking in his boots. The road had disappeared, they were walking along planks to prevent them sinking into the mud. A muddy, dirty, exhausted platoon carrying an assortment of miscellaneous equipment staggered into view. These were the men they were replacing. A last wild look around the nightmare landscape and they left their plank walk and leapt down into the trenches.

These were deep, floored with planks, in places with muddy water to splash through; at intervals were dugouts and opposite steps cut in the wall, and a tin-hatted soldier keeping watch. Barbed-wire entanglements covered several yards; a few blood-stained bodies decaying from the last sortie, and seas of mud with deep shell holes flooded with water were the only things in sight. The sun still shone mercilessly, but he felt cold with horror. Heavy bombardment with shells started up. So this was the front line. The sergeant gave the order to brew up. After a hot cuppa was in his hands, he relaxed and in a day or so, trench life in all its damp muddy discomfort and danger became a normal way of existence.

One of my friends had a German mother. In the 1930s we went on holiday to Germany to stay with her relatives. Betty was already there with a Scot, and I travelled out with another half-German cousin to join them. Hitler had just had one of his great 'Strength with Joy' rallies. Everywhere we went, the German youth were full of praise for his movement – joining up fast. Chrissie, as a Scot, was cautious in her views about this, and so was I. Privately we both thought the adulation was a bit hysterical. Back home no one in London seemed to take much notice. Pity!

After the Abdication in the 1930s, Britain went through all the stages of grief, shock and finally abandonment. The nation had been used to Princes of Wales having mistresses throughout a long history, but Kings had never abandoned the throne so speedily to marry someone considered unworthy. It was natural to feel first sadness, and then indignation.

The new King took the name George VI and it was decided by the government to have the Coronation as soon as possible, much the same date as it would have been for Edward VIII. A holiday was announced for this day.

My flatmate went home for this, but I was alone when a friend came in and suggested after the broadcast that it would be a good idea to go over to Hyde Park and watch the procession. Park Lane was crowded but we stood on a slight rise under some trees in the park and got a reasonable view. I remember best the open carriage with the stately Queen Mary and two excited small princesses wearing coronets on their fair curls.

With no TV then, this brief glimpse of a great royal occasion was all the people had, apart from newspaper pictures and film shows the next day. For the next Coronation, most people viewed the whole procedure on the small screen. Television from that day on would mirror the world's greatest events into one's own sitting room. I wonder sometimes if this is a good idea. For my part, I have always liked to be part of the crowd excitingly getting a glimpse of the procession just as other people have done on all such occasions. I went to watch King George VI's funeral procession, and again stood behind the crowd on a rise under trees, in Green Park, Piccadilly, this time, because of my fear of fainting. It had not been a really long reign, about 14 years, but a marvellous occasion. The crowd showed great feeling. One felt they were giving thanks for a difficult task well done.

In 1938 the prospect of war with Germany was uncomfortably close. The issue of gas masks caused a shudder of anticipation. In 1939 war was declared in September; the sirens sounded almost as the Prime Minister ended his speech. We had already watched the heart-rending scene of the evacuation of children from the capital to the countryside. No one really understood what life was going to be like in the years to come. But immediately we realised that the King and Queen would play their part. Some children were being shipped to safety in Canada and America, but the Queen announced that she could not leave the King, and of course the princesses would stay with their parents.

It seems to me that all wars are different and only people who have lived through them know what they are like. There has been plenty of material written about World War II so historians can paint an accurate picture. After the initial shock of the declaration of war, the evacuation of children from London and the larger towns, calling up reserves, and people joining the colours, we settled down to what was called a 'phony war'. News came of faraway disasters, blackouts were put in place and diligently regulated by the ARP, but it was not until the summer of 1940 that the appalling shock of the fall of France and Dunkirk, followed by devastating air raids, brought realisation of what this war was going to be like. Great Britain stood alone supported by Empire, ill equipped after so many army supplies had to be abandoned in France when the remnants of the army had been brought home by that amazing flotilla of pleasure boats assisting the Royal Navy in its tremendous task. It was the air force with the gallant lively young pilots who had to fight the Luftwaffe in the Battle of Britain while resources were built up to carry on. Air raids caused heavy civilian casualties.

One surprise from total war was the incredible beautiful paintings it inspired; the bombed derelict churches, immortalised by John Piper; the sight of burning buildings, leaping flames; searchlights quartering the sky seeking targets; well-known buildings outlined by fire, their reflection in the Thames – the list is endless.

Once war has ended, there is no point in looking back. One has to get on with living, but there is one memory that sometimes flashes across my mind. It concerns an incendiary bomb raid, I was on leave, staying with my father at home, fire-watching, as Stepmother was on duty at her Red Cross Hospital. An enemy plane flew low above the hills that blocked our view of Bristol.

99

In the valley below the railway emerged from a deep cutting. There was a bank planted with fir trees along the track; the plane jettisoned its cargo of fire bombs and they fell among the trees. It had been snowing and as the bombs burst into flames as they hit the ground, the dark fir trees were illuminated by thousands of stars, reds, yellows, mauves and an incandescent green.

There is a recurring dream that still sometimes wakes me in the night. I am standing on a table in Hodgson's Yard, Eton. Mary Francis stands behind me, shining a torch onto the white pages of a book as it is blackout. I am taking roll-call for the WRNS. They dash out of one door of Hodgson House and into the next. An air raid is in progress; the German planes are flying back from London, dropping any bombs left over from their raid. There is a noisy barrage from our anti-aircraft guns and some shrapnel patters down. Sometimes my shout is drowned by these noises off and I have to pause. At last my job is done and I can go in to report to the WRNS officer and check if any blanks on my register are on sudden compassionate leave.

This dream wakes me and I lie in bed wondering where the hell so-and-so has got to, and worry if she has been injured or even killed, and slowly I realise that this all happened in 1941 or 42 when stationed at Eton, with quarters at Hodgson House, the opposite side of the road to the college. The house is still there, no longer called Hodgson. Two and a half times as many Wrens lived there as boys, the previous residents, had numbered, so we were very cramped.

A few years ago, I went back to Eton on a visit and could not resist opening the door into the yard. It still looked the same but I could not see if the door the other side was still the entrance to Pop, the boys' famous club.

When I was demobbed in 1946, both food and clothing were still rationed, and every sort of household goods on short supply. Winston Churchill, our wartime leader, was defeated in the first peacetime election and a Labour Government took over with Clement Atlee as Prime Minister. Princess Elizabeth married the Duke of Edinburgh and Charles and Anne were born. The King became ill, so the Princess took over the arranged tour to South Africa. He looked very frail in the newspaper photographs as he waved goodbye to his daughter, Sadly he died at Sandringham in his sleep. The news was broken to the Princess that she was now Queen, and the photographs of the time showed her coming down the aircraft steps to be greeted as Queen by Winston Churchill, who had become Prime Minister again.

The Coronation next year established television, as I have mentioned. For the first time, not only her subjects, but the world, would be able to watch on the small screen as the Queen was being crowned in Westminster Abbey. There was a great demand for TV sets. My brother-in-law had a large TV installed and the family spent all day watching the ceremony.

The Queen is nearing her 50th anniversary on the throne. Her dedication to her duty has won the admiration and affection of her subjects. It is sad that the marriages of her children have taken on the pattern of the current behaviour of many young people. Parents and grandparents recognised her mention of her *annus horribilis*. Many of them have and will have the same experience. Freedom and openness in affairs of sex seem to be the spirit of the times. Newspapers flourish by publishing sleaze. After all, they replace the broadsheets of old that flourished in the streets of London from time immemorial.

My sympathies go to the children of broken homes. They are the real sufferers at any age. I can imagine their feelings at the taunts of their schoolfellows, their divided loyalties, the sense of being in a tug of war between parents. My stepmama, when she was running a boarding school just after the war, when the first batches of children from divorced homes arrived, said very practically, 'I put them in the dormitory with others who have gone through the hoop. They are the best comforters, they tell of two Christmases, two birthday treats and lots of extra outings.' I was doubtful then, and later found when letting to students that the young suffer even when they are old enough to understand the reasons for the break-up of their home.

Politicians are now prating of 'family values'. Schools are moaning about unruly, unteachable pupils. It would be interesting to know how many of these children come from broken homes and unmarried mothers. Both parents and teachers suffer from no sanctions to offer. It is of course horrifying to hear of children ill-treated, but in my young days, my brothers and myself were smacked when naughty, and the boys were beaten at school for wrongdoing. One learnt not to repeat the offence. Now there is talk of a law to make parents of children under the age of ten responsible for their crimes; fining them money? Children should learn what is right and what is wrong-doing before they go to school.

Way back in the 1950s William Beveridge launched the Welfare State. At the time it sounded wonderful. We were to be looked after from the cradle to the grave – to be financed by insurance from all workers. Even then I had my doubts. As soon as I had saved the then magnificent sum, to me, of £1,000, mostly by selling my designs, I got an introduction to my father's stockbroker and began investing on the Stock Exchange. My first buy was Shell, and I still have a modest amount of their shares today.

In the 1950s no one could have foreseen the wonderful progress of medical science. There seems to be an operation now for most disasters, all requiring expensive surgery. Many illnesses have almost disappeared by inoculation and injection – these have all ensured that more people live longer. National Health makes enormous demands on the Welfare State. The pattern of industry has changed by invention too. Computers and machines can be run by fewer people so have caused unemployment. Fewer manual workers are needed and more highly trained individuals. Research into everything is now current. Inflation has caused everyone to demand higher pay. Modern living standards mean we all want more equipment to make life easier, but it all costs money.

Family patterns have changed, too. In my young days, five children was not unusual – quite a change from the eight to fifteen of earlier centuries. Now 'two and a half' is considered the norm. Birth control has brought about this change and the Pill has given women choice about when they want to have a child. Unfortunately they have to remember to take it regularly – a task apparently difficult for some girls. Beveridge never could have visualised the numbers of unmarried mothers the state has to provide for today. It takes a male and a female to produce a baby (though scientists today have 'cloned' a lamb, so their next ambition will be to clone a human); it should be the father's job to support mother and child. The government rather belatedly recognised this a year or two ago but it has become a slow progress to trace the fathers and then make them pay maintenance, as many have acquired a new family for whom they have to provide.

Children of all ages need both parents: they also need a happy home for their first few years. In many homes divorce has robbed them of their birthright. Nowadays about one-third of all marriages end in divorce. No wonder that schools are beginning to suffer from 'unteachable' children who provoke havoc and even attack their teachers; what sanctions do the teachers now have to enforce discipline?

Just after the Second World War, I was lodging with two friends. A cousin of theirs came to stay and they were reticent about her employment. However, she was full of chat about her job. An ex-sergeant in the ATS, she was in charge of a home for single pregnant girls. They came in at seven months, they were treated kindly and medically correctly until they gave birth, allowed to convalesce with their baby for a month, then a society arranged for the baby to be adopted. The girl was directed to a job and her space in the home filled by another in waiting. I enquired if they ever got the same girl back again. 'Well yes, sometimes,' the cousin admitted. 'But we are not so nice to her second time round.'

A few years later, I went to an international fair in Brussels and because all hotels were full, stayed in the wing of a convent. This belonged to a beautiful house in its own park, with a lake. I love gardens, particularly historic ones, and wandering around I met the Mother Superior. She befriended me and told me all about the convent. The wing that housed the foreign visitors to the fair was the 'naughty' girls' home. It was they who waited on us at breakfast and dinner. The nuns nursed them, minded the babies and sent the girls out daily to suitable jobs. On Saturday night there was a dance, and suitable young men came. The nuns fostered romances, and in due course would provide a trousseau and a wedding if a girl found a fiancé. Again the baby would probably go for adoption. The practical nuns realised that few men take to a baby in the home that is not their own. How attitudes have changed in little more than 50 years.

There have been other changes too. When I was born, governments varied between Liberal and Conservative; Labour as a party did not exist until the Great War. Then in the 1920s Ramsey MacDonald became the first Labour Prime Minister. From then on, the government has swung between Conservative and Labour. We had a coalition for the Second World War, but Attlee was elected for the peace. One sure thing is that everyone has always ended up suffering financially when Labour leaves office. Eighteen years of Tory rule are at an end. Eighteen year-olds who had never had a Labour government could vote in the election on 1 May 1997. Perhaps it is only fair for Labour to have their turn to govern. People have short memories but at 90 years old I can look back at a series of Labour governments that one and all left the country impoverished.

There was a time in the late 1950s and early 1960s when dread of a nuclear war caused the young to feel they must have everything they wanted *now*, as their lives would be short. This generation is now in its fifties and sixties but that is possibly an inherited pattern for overindulging children to this day, and fortunately a World War III has never happened.

There have been wars since the Second World War; the Suez Canal was said to flow through Anthony Eden's drawing room, and that brought his career as Prime Minister to an end. There was the invasion of the Falklands and the Gulf War as localised warfare. Troops have been sent on peace-making duties to Yugoslavia and other parts of the world. It seems that there is always war somewhere in this world even if it does not act as a touchstone for a major conflict.

Perhaps the most significant happening in the twentieth century was America winning the space race to put a man on the moon. The night before this happened I went into the garden and gazed up at the moon, thinking of all the romance and poetry through the ages that it had inspired. Would all this be lost when we could all see the dreary grey expanse of moon rock? Watching with wonder as the spaceman crept down the ladder from the space rocket, his helmet and space suit looked familiar; there was a sudden remembrance of comics in our nursery long ago. How did those newspaper artists foresee the shape of things to come?

Space travel and exploration continues. Astronauts have spent a year in space; sometimes tied to their craft by a lifeline, they float around mending outside equipment. We watch on our TV sets; people occasionally wonder aloud if all this travel through the ozone layer is producing enough holes to increase global warming, but are generally reassured. Exhaust fumes from cars and factories are usually condemned as the culprits. It seems another far-off age since our greatest treat was a ride in Grandpa's car, sometimes the only one on the road, when any delays were caused by flocks of sheep, or herds of cows being taken back to the farm for milking.

9

Reflections

Ninety years have passed since I was born. Those years have included five reigns, two world wars and the suffragette movement, plus numerous inventions which have changed everyone's domestic life. Take transport; I can remember horses and carts, elegant pony traps drive with dash by young matrons and their younger sisters. Older people owned carriages drawn by a pair of horses, works outings travelled in 'brakes', narrow carts lined with two long seats facing one another. There was a curved top of iron hoops over which a tarpaulin could be drawn if it rained. Strips hung from this roof and when the brakes returned from their day at the sea, many of the occupants were strap-hanging, dancing and singing the popular songs of the day. They had made a few stops on the way for refreshment at inns. Popular songs were known by all; errand boys sang them as they cycled round on deliveries – with a large box over the bicycle's front wheel; our nanny sang them to us on our walks and when we were bathed – 'If you were the only girl in the world and I was the only boy' or 'Daisy, Daisy, give me your answer do' or 'Tipperary'. The sound of these brings those faraway days back to me. Without radio and television, people had to make their own amusements. They played cards, billiards and other games. An evening party usually finished up with everyone singing around the piano. The children, woken from sleep, would hang over the banisters upstairs, enjoying the music until they climbed back into their beds and slipped back into sleep with those tunes ringing in their ears.

In the summers, we went on picnics – picked wild daffodils, white violets and cowslips in their season, then as autumn approached we went blackberrying or gathering hazelnuts. Life was never dull. When we were taken to Cambridge to stay with our grandparents, our young uncles and aunts organised river picnics for us all.

At my mother's home, brother Norman and myself were allowed to trundle metal hoops along the pavement, down the next little street, turn left at the bottom of the hill, then right again and so home. The hoops made a splendid sound as they bounced over the paving stones. Aubrey, at three years old, was considered to be too young to take part in such delights and by the time he was old enough baby Peggy had joined the nursery, and we did not visit Cambridge so much. We managed, however, to have most of our childhood illnesses like measles, chicken pox, etc. at Cambridge. When one child in the family caught an infectious disease they put the others in with him to ensure they all got over it before school days began. I can recall well the 'measly' room and lying in bed itching, trying not to scratch and having three guesses with my brothers and cousin as to what our paternal grandfather would bring us when he came home for lunch. He was a great big jolly man who loved children and never let us down. We must have been a nuisance to my aunt and my mother, but perhaps it was better for them to share the load together.

When we were free from infection we children had breakfast and lunch with our grandparents and mother and father. We sat on one side of the table, perched on stools – I sat next to my little gran, then came cousin Kenneth, brothers Norman and Aubrey. Children were meant to be seen but not heard; we were not supposed to speak unless invited. Grown-ups were inclined to sit talking at meals so when we children had finished eating our pudding, one of the mothers would say to my little gran, 'May the children get down now?' and then we ran off happily to our playroom.

Years later at Sunday lunch with my friends Con and David, when their children had been noisy and difficult, David turned to me and said, 'Was it the rule children should be seen and not heard at meals in your home?'

"Grandpa's Taxi" 1910

I replied of course it was, and young Sue, aged five, at once protested, 'Not fair, not fair – how absolutely unfair!'

Grandpa had a motor car about 1910. It was upholstered in heavy grey cord material trimmed with braid. On the partition between passengers and the driver Dave was a cut-glass vase. This always seemed to hold a carnation, pale pink if my little gran was a passenger, rich dark red for my aunt Maud.

One Easter, when the family was visiting us, Father and Mother, Uncle Jack and Auntie Maud took all four children to Clevedon, a nearby seaside resort. Kenneth, Norman, Aubrey and myself were put on the small jetty pier and told to be good while the grown-ups went for a walk. We soon got bored with this small pier and clambered down to the beach. The tide was going out; Clevedon has practically no beach but the outgoing tide left gorgeous rich dark Bristol Channel mud. We had a lovely time playing with this, scooping it up to make water channels, falling over in the lovely squishy soft blackness. When the grown-ups returned there were screams of horror from Mama and Maudie. Only Father took an interest in our waterways. While all the horrified scolding was going on, the resourceful Uncle Jack had quietly crossed the road to the newsagent's and acquired a heap of out-of-date newspapers. We were mopped down with these then turned into newspaper parcels so that we would not dirty that beautiful upholstery.

Transport and traffic has been completely revolutionised since those early days. In due course we all had bicycles to get to school. Aubrey had a cast-off model from Clifton friends, called Julius Caesar. This was very well known in Clifton and he was often stopped by young men wanting to try and ride on what had once been their transport.

Later the boys progressed to motor bikes and I became a pillion rider. Then our youngest aunt, Margery, newly married, and husband Ron came to stay with their proud possession, a Morgan run-about. This was a three-wheeled car. Margery decided to show off and take me for a drive. We drove along our driveway in style but we both got out to open the gates and the car took wings and began to roll down steep Golf Lane. Shrieking with a mixture of laughter and terror, we chased after it, and Marge managed to reach in for the handbrake. We did continue with our expedition, rather chastened by the thought of the car dashing down the rest of the hill to the main road if Margery hadn't managed to grab the brake. Mother dissolved in laughter when we returned with our tale but firmly forbade us to tell anyone else.

Eventually Father bought a large Armstrong Siddely tourer to ferry the family around.

Now aircraft were being developed and every young man's ambition was to learn to fly.

There was rivalry on the railways as to which had the best dinner menu. The LMS food was perhaps the best, the GWR was more reliable, the LNER was noted for something else while the Somerset and Dorset was reckoned to live up to its nickname 'Slow and Dirty'. These of course were all steam trains, and made unforgettable noises as they got up power – 'I think I can, I think I can – I thought I could, I thought I could' was the chant we sang happily to the rhythm.

During the Second World War petrol was severely rationed for private use – there was little traffic on roads apart from army lorries and goods vehicles.

I do recall thinking that the Welfare State that came into being after the war had been a rushed business and many problems had not been foreseen. How right this view was. No one then guessed what this new medical triumph the 'Pill' would mean. Women now had the chance to choose a possible date for the birth of a child. One suspects that all down the centuries there had been trials of birth control methods, some fairly successful, some not. The 'Pill' has one great disadvantage: one has to remember to take it regularly for it to be sure to work, as many a scatty girl has found to her cost. Otherwise, why so high an abortion rate? Dangerous pregnancies cannot account for all of them.

Sex education is now taught in schools. At first it was a trifle inadequate, disguised often as human biology. Some parents gleaned a little scientific knowledge from their children's 'Hum. B.' notebooks surreptitiously overnight. I suspect the first generation of teachers, poor dears, felt too embarrassed to remember to stress that this was one lesson where the pupils were not to do homework – judging from the numbers of schoolgirl pregnancies. 'Found under the gooseberry bushes' had never seemed an adequate answer to 'where babies come from'. My sex education, not really needed for a country child, was completed when my brothers first went to prep school and brought home an illustrated copy of Marie Stopes. They felt it only right that their sister should know the 'facts of life'. The only drawback to this was a very embarrassing interview with Mother years later when she attempted to enlighten the three of us on this subject. We felt, poor dear, she was not very professional.

It seemed before the First World War, when a young lady broke the unwritten rules and became pregnant, she was hastily sent to the Continent with a convenient maiden aunt 'to finish her education'. Eventually the 'little mistake' was suitably adopted and she returned home to re-enter the marriage market. The war put an end to this convenient practice because there was no foreign country to which one could travel. Village girls were more fortunate; everyone crowded up a little more and Mum sometimes had her own baby and her erring daughter's in the same pram.

Two world wars modified people's views. It was too hard to refuse someone going to the front with a good chance that he would be killed before his next leave. There were tragedies in the WRNS like this. When America joined us in World War II, quite a few GI brides were not prepared to go and live in what was to them a strange country; some returned and some found they had taken on a man already married.

Mothers who had had babies in the Second World War had another unexpected problem when Dad was demobilised and returned home. Many children did not welcome this large stranger taking up Mum's attention and getting all the scarce treats previously always reserved for their enjoyment. Fathers sometimes found their offspring tiresome and spoilt, and obviously poor tired overworked Mum was not the lively young girl they had married.

This Second World War was very different from the First World War. Then in 1914 most young men had rushed to enlist. Young officers barely trained were slaughtered by enemy fire as they led their troops to battle from the trenches.

That war changed life for women more than the suffragette movement had done. In my early childhood the grown-ups had discussed the 'outrageous' idea that women should have the vote. Mother laughed and said she would like one. In the 1920s I had the vote, but although I have dutifully voted on all occasions, it has seemed an obligation rather than a privilege.

One aspect of life today has changed completely: that is health. With getting old I have become a little frail and have begun to sample the National Health. It absolutely horrifies me to hear the grumbles and complaints of the majority of my fellow users. Don't they realise that they are getting the benefits of today's medical science and knowledge free? I know as workers we paid a nominal sum to contribute to the Welfare State but this could never foot the bill for what is being done.

In our village the doctor managed tactfully to charge a reasonable fee to those who lived in big houses and were monied, and treated the cottagers free. It worked well. My mother was an invalid and our doctor was a great friend and bridge partner of hers. Finding her stranded without her bridge at one of the Research Station dances, I asked where the doctor was. 'Oh,' she said, 'Jinny Mitchell is dying and Gordon has gone to see her out.' Jinny, our old charwoman, was an ancient character who had been staging deathbed scenes for quite a few years, but this one was genuine. Gordon returned an hour or so later, depressed but pleased he had fulfilled his promise and closed Jinny's eyes. This would have been about 1927 and Jinny would have been in her late eighties. I am the same age now, and although medical science has produced so many marvellous operations and treatments, they are all incredibly expensive. One begins to wonder whether it is sensible to operate on the elderly to give them the chance of a few more years, or whether they should be reserved for the young with years of life ahead. With such a large proportion of people living longer, this problem will have to be resolved eventually.

Courtship and marriage have also changed completely during my lifetime. When my aunts reached the age of 17 or 18 they put up their hair, had a few new dresses and 'came out'. This meant they were taken to parties and dances and to pay calls. Mothers had been collecting young men as suitable guests for these parties for some time, and the result was the girls who knew they were expected to get engaged and then married had a good look around for a suitable partner. The usual prize was a man five to ten years older in a suitable job who would be able to keep them in their accustomed style. Most seemed to achieve this in a year or two. There were a few who found an unsuitable candidate and even went so far as to elope with him. The unlucky ones eventually were spoken of as 'on the shelf!' and could only look forward to a life of caring for their aged parents – or holding sisters' hands when they had a baby and running their households.

The village girls and working classes had perhaps more freedom of choice, though they too fancied a steady young man even though it meant they 'walked out' for several years until he earned enough to provide a home.

The First World War changed this pattern for ever. One reason was the slaughter of young men – the casualty lists were enormous. Another was that girls were needed to work in munitions factories and shops to replace men who were called up as the war progressed. At the ending, parents probably hoped the old systems would return but the young had ideas of their own.

112

Nevertheless, when I left school most of my form who didn't go to university got engaged, mostly suitably, and married fairly soon – although there was a shortage of older men available. One or two got genteel jobs. With my sister Peggy's form seven years later it was completely different; they were all taking up training for jobs as a matter of course because the 1930s were the time of the Depression and great unemployment. Girls who lived away from home still took their young men home for parental approval, which was usually forthcoming. Marriage was mostly looked upon as lasting for life.

The 1939–45 war again brought changes. There were many widows around looking for a new husband and plenty of GI brides – some of whom settled, some of whom disliked America and came home. Divorce was more difficult in 1945. A few couples could not settle down after a long separation, but the majority stayed together. Marriage was still regarded as an unbreakable contract made in church. I have noticed that my married friends who stayed together, perhaps weathering a few stormy passages on the way, have had a happier old age than those who could not turn a blind eye.

It seems today that marriage is no longer the goal of the young. Though divorce is much easier now, it is a trying and expensive experience, so why not live with your partner and split up when you do not see eye to eye over the details of daily living? The problem comes when there is a family. Children need both parents in every way. There is no age at which they do not suffer.

I remember a friend married to a man divorced from his first wife with three children. He had a good job, but the first wife was always asking for more money to pay the children's dentist etc. My friend kept on her job but was often highly indignant about these demands, saying she was working to keep someone else's children while postponing one of her own. This was about the 1980s.

There are now many unmarried mothers and I feel worried and sorry for their children. Whatever the mothers do or say, that child is disadvantaged not living in a balanced home. Children need a mother and a father. They learn from observing them, and their reactions to every situation. Of course a father should support his offspring. In my young day people had large families – we were five – and so they learnt from one another. It is right that men should pay for the upbringing of their children and not leave it to the Welfare State. It is a father's responsibility, even if he is separated or divorced.

School cannot do the duties of parents, and has a right to have children with basic training and awareness of what is right and what wrong. Standards of behaviour should be learnt in the home.

It seems unfortunate that schools have given up prayers each morning. I know the difficulties in a multi-racial society, but surely a simple prayer and hymn could be non-denominational. Marching and standing in line with one's form taught self-control and discipline, and encouraged the feeling that one was part of a community. I was not allowed to go to prayers because I was likely to fall flat in a faint, but felt a bit of an outcast over this. School games are needed too as they provide healthy competition and an opportunity for children to let off steam. Thank goodness schools are returning to games for all.

As a young teenager I played truant every Thursday afternoon with a schoolfriend to go to the matinee at Bristol's Old Vic Theatre down in the docks. Even in those days I was keen on art so the school authorities must have thought I was at extra art in the studio. I was quite clever and able to keep up with whatever subjects I was skipping. My friend Biddy was older than myself, a clergyman's daughter. I seem to remember her excuse was 'extra coaching'. She was never bright at lessons. Our theatre going came to an end when she eloped with a married man – horrors! Biddy was expelled, my parents were warned to keep a stricter eye on me. I took myself to the studio on Thursday afternoons and was quite glad to be moved back from the parallel form to the School Certificate form at the end of term.

Nowadays truancy has become a general problem for schools. I am sorry for teachers. How they deal with wrongdoers when they have no sanctions, one can't imagine. In my day, we were given 'careless returns' and had to stay in on half-holidays to write out one or more hundred lines. We thought our brothers were luckier in being beaten! There were no drugs around. Our

114

worst crime seemed to be having a puff at an illicit cigarette behind the bicycle sheds. There was little interest to me in that game as my brothers and I had been taught to smoke by Sonny Griffiths, our gardener's boy, years ago!

Reading the press tales of juvenile delinquents, violence in the classroom, let alone in the playground, frequent truancies, all point to the fact that 'family values' must be restored. One rather wonders how.

10

First Overseas Tour – August 1970: Australia and New Zealand

Late August 1970, I set off by sea to Australia and New Zealand, where I was to give lectures and run workshops. Going by sea was my retirement treat as I had always envied the sailors on my ledgers as a Wren, and now was my opportunity to visit many of the ports that had once been familiar voices on the telephone.

It was a round-the-world trip, coming back via the Far East and the Panama Canal. I then thought it would be a one off expedition, but before sailing home New Zealand had arranged a Queen Elizabeth II grant to fund a second trip in 1972. There was also to be a third journey in America and Canada in 1974.

A voyage is not like a cruise. The ship becomes a home. The people at your table are a substitute family and days at sea follow an easy routine. Breakfast, walk round the deck, keep-fit class, coffee; for myself then, work on the warps and drafts to be posted from the next port to Australia and New Zealand. Then a swim in the pool, buffet lunch on the top deck, siesta and sunbathe, another swim, tea, Scrabble or bridge or concert, change for dinner then perhaps a film, or cabaret or dance, and next day repeat the whole performance. It is never boring as the sea and sky are endlessly changing and there are new friends to make. One is given talks about the next port; then visits of discovery are exciting treats, but as soon as the ship sails out of harbour the usual daily pattern of life returns.

After Fremantle all this pattern changed. Some friends

disembarked at their journey's end and were to be replaced by noisy newcomers; Australians who were travelling to Sydney, where the ship would turn into a cruise liner for several months before returning to the UK. My cabin companions left for their homes at the port of Adelaide. One of them had been in the sickbay after a heart attack, so I spent my shore leave going to her home and meeting her family. Her son had played rugger for Wales before emigrating. He longed to hear about Twickenham and the international rugger matches, and even the varsity match. This was my first glimpse of the homesickness for the country that they had left. Later I met several British people who had retired to Australia to settle near their children and grandchildren, but they all talked wistfully of the village or town they had left behind. They missed their old friends.

The ship put into the port of Melbourne for a day and a half, so I was able to go shopping. I wanted to buy petticoats, which I had left behind in my hasty packing just before I sailed. Finally we reached Sydney. I was up at daybreak as we passed the Heads and entered the harbour. The naval chapel stands central with its great window behind the altar looking out to sea. Later I was taken to visit it and felt that in its simplicity standing on the headland it was the right memorial to all sailors lost at sea.

My Australian friends were busy pointing out all the landmarks, the different places round the shore and the creeks. It seemed an immense inland sea before the sails of the opera house roof hove into view. Behind this the Harbour Bridge was silhouetted, and one could easily see why they called it the 'Coathanger'. On the right hand side of the harbour was Cremorne, with the landing stage at the edge of the creek. I was to make headquarters in a small private hotel there called the Bokara. A friend had booked me a room there for the first weekend in Australia. In the midst of disembarking, going through the entrance formalities, I was called on the tannoy. I found that the local Guild Secretary, Eve Rashleigh, had come to meet me. She drove me across the bridge to the Bokara and suggested that she collected me early the next morning to take me into the country, where she and her friend Sylvia owned a craft shop. We were then to sleep overnight in a caravan before driving nearly to

Canberra to a sheep farm to see the shearing. This was a great welcome, and I enjoyed the camping immensely.

It got hotter and hotter as we drove across rough ground to the shearing shed. The skinny white merinos were crowding to the little creek that ran through their pen. In the shed it was hardly possible to breathe. The shearers, stripped to the waist and shiny with sweat, were working at a terrific pace. As each fleece was ready the farmer did a quick check before tossing it into one of several large mesh containers. It suddenly dawned on me that this sort might have something to do with Bradford quality numbers. I dared to have a guess. Luckily this was near enough to the correct number. The farmer was pleased with me and so were Eve and Sylvia; my credentials were established thanks to Leeds University Textile Department.

The next day as I was to fly to New Zealand for a fortnight of lecture workshops, the hotel agreed to keep some luggage for me and booked a room for my return. I had already fallen in love with Cremorne. The hotel's garden with orange and lemon trees opened onto the reserve; a green walk, on the top of a rocky cliff, leading to the ferry station. One could climb down to the creek where there was a sailing club. Toronga, Sydney's zoo, was silhouetted against the sky and at the point there was a delightful small Victorian lighthouse. The granddaughter of the man who designed it was to be one of my pupils. What a wonderful way to go to work – to walk under the flowering trees to the ferry then 15 minutes crossing the harbour with splendid views of the opera house and the bridge to left and right. The ferry had to avoid ships of every size, from sailing dinghies to liners. Sometimes it could be windy and rough – rough enough on these days to look forward to safe arrival at Circular Quay. There were rush-hour travellers and businessmen taking this trip as calmly as their fellows in London go on the underground to the City. Up the hill on the right was a place where early settlers built their delightful stone cottages in Regency–Victorian style. My workplace lay straight ahead, a walk between skyscrapers to the top floor of a tall building overlooking the park. After a day in which I felt the heat badly, it was always good to get back to home in Cremorne. There, there was an open-air swimming pool carved out of the rocky cliff, with water renewed every day by the tide. Eve frightened me with a tale that once a baby shark was found there, having managed to swim up the inlet. It was no wonder that Sydney became my home town on both visits to Australia. I returned to Cremorne each time like a homing pigeon.

The flight to New Zealand was completely different from any of my experience with holiday flights to Europe. I was talking to a young New Zealander as we walked across the tarmac to board the plane when a steward came up and said, 'Your rifle, please, sir. I must lock it in the kitchen.' I found this slightly startling, but the reason became obvious when we settled into our seats. The traveller on my other side was an elderly English lady. She and her husband had visited their daughter in New Zealand earlier in the year. Unfortunately he died, so she went back home, sold up her house and was returning with this flight to settle near her daughter. Her journey coincided with the first dramatic hijack of an airliner in the desert. We had heard about this in newsflashes on our liner, so it was very interesting to hear details. Airports were all, understandably, nervous and each time her aircraft landed she was subjected to a body search. Sydney was the first exception. It seemed that she took it quite calmly, but it must have been a shock to someone like herself that everyone on the airliner was under suspicion.

Another of our fellow travellers had five small children with her: a baby in arms, whose cradle was hung on the front of the plane just behind the pilot's cabin, a toddler who needed constant attention from a worried little seven-year-old sister, and a diabolical pair of twins, five-year-old boys who played merry hell. They would charge up and down the gangway, upsetting the stewards serving lunch; their favourite pastime was to turn a series of somersaults clutching the backs of seats down the aisle. At last the pilot himself, a resourceful man, came out, and taking each twin by an ear said, 'Come with me, fellows, and I will show you how to fly the plane.' Peace at last until two chastened boys came back to Mummy.

Wellington Airport has the reputation of being wild and windy. We certainly had a bumpy descent. All five children screamed piercingly at the top of their voices, adding to the nervous discomfort of us all. Not a reassuring beginning to my first job in New Zealand.

I said goodbye to my fellow travellers who had been so friendly during my long flight and felt like a forlorn left-luggage parcel waiting collection. This feeling was to become very familiar during the next nine months because the arrangements had been that I would be paid a fee for lectures and workshops, but given accommodation, usually by a Guild member, for the duration of the workshop. At every new place there was uncertainty about where I would stay and would they remember to meet me. Actually, in practice this worked very well. Everyone was most hospitable, showed me all the sights, and I got a much more informed impression of life in New Zealand and Australia than I would have had if I had always stayed at hotels.

At Wellington Airport it was not a long wait before Lady Turner, wife of the Appeals Court Judge, collected me. Wellington is built on hills and their house was one where the living rooms were on top, parallel with the drive, to get the magnificent view over the bay towards South Island, and then downstairs were the bedrooms. The Judge had cooked us an appetising meal that I was almost too tired to eat. Lady Turner filled me in about my programme, which started the next day. The looms were all set up ready, which was a comfort. She sent me off promptly to bed, saying I was to sleep in the room last occupied by the Lord Chancellor of England. It was a charming room, looking out onto the downhill garden, but what struck me most was a wonderful hand-woven rug in yellow and white rolags of fleece held by an open warp. It looked so fragile that I avoided stepping on it when climbing into bed and moved it to a safe position. Lady Turner laughed at this when she woke me next morning and said she put it in the washing tub between visitors, shook the water out and it dried as good as new.

That first workshop in New Zealand was an ordeal. The Guild had considered my drafts and the order of threading of yarns of mixed colour distinctly unconventional. I had to deal with a certain amount of prejudice before we settled down to work and got results.

The plan was for everyone to make a 4–6 inch sample in the

regular weave for that draft, then to make a second sample lifting the shafts in any order that they chose, out of the combination of lifts – 14 altogether on 4 shafts; namely plain weave – that's two, two and two twill, four lifts, one and three and three and one twills eight lifts. The main difficulty in this kind of lesson was that speeds of weaving varied. There was always someone who did not want anyone else to weave on their loom. Then unfortunately some warps did not weave too well, possibly because of the loom, possibly because the yarns weren't quite suitable. There were always a few threading errors or reed mistakes to correct. This meant the first morning was hectic, rushing from loom to loom unless I had had time to check the looms beforehand. It was always important to stress that it was better to have two good samples on two different warps, four in all, than to rush round having a go on six or seven looms and finishing up with uselessly small fraying samples when they were all cut up and divided. I stressed the paperwork must be copied accurately and they all noted carefully the order of lifted shafts in their own individual sample. I had prepared cards with full weaving details to hang on each loom and just had to check they copied these accurately. They were asked to put their names on the list to say which loom they hoped to try next. If there were going to be more than 12 looms, I duplicated some drafts to speed up changes. When I did this duplication of drafts I usually chose two entirely different yarns for the warps. This was a useful way of showing the different behaviour of fibres, because when we had finished at the end of the workshop, I cut all the warps off and gave them a textile wet finish before we divided them up, so that they could see how the finished fabric should look.

I had adopted this type of workshop very early in my teaching career because I had been shocked how little hand weavers experimented with cloth structure. In my time at Leeds University we all had warps that we practised on and tried every sort of variation. Early in the GJ's existence I had done a goodwill tour round the Guilds giving talks on contemporary weaving with slides and my own samples first, then ending with promoting the *Journal*, discussing what they wanted from it, and giving them an opportunity to air their complaints. Always on these occasions someone brought up a sleazy sample and said, 'I copied this exactly from the book and it doesn't look like the picture.' They had not understood that it never would unless they used the same size of yarn, same ends per inch in warp and weft as the illustration. Very often the author had woven her sample in exaggerated, unusually thick yarns in black and white so the photographs would be clear. Their difficulties in understanding this problem had convinced me it was a good idea to try out workshops to promote proper choice of yarn and sett.

My favourite drafts for a workshop were two for straight entry, one in a tweed singles yarn for coatings, suitings etc. and one in two twelves mercerised cotton. This was useful for curtains and other furnishings. Then I had some of the traditional ones such as Rosepath, Honeysuckle, Blooming Flower, Swedish Lace, Waffle, then Double Corduroy, Double Cloth and Extra Warp. These last three were to show some of the more advanced fabrics possible to weave on four shafts only.

My first workshop must have been a success. There were two sisters there who had to be steered from very conventional samples. On the last day they presented me with a pound of New Zealand wool that they had spun during the evenings. When I got home it was knitted up carefully into a large sweater; actually I am wearing this while writing. Another present was a beret knitted in unspun wool, a type of roving.

My next stop was to be Hamilton on the way to Auckland. My policy Down Under was to travel by road or train so that I could see as much of the countryside as possible, so I went up by the luxury Landliner coach. This had a hostess, a drinks bar also serving hot tea and coffee, and a loo. We were given a commentary about places we passed by the hostess. Very soon after we had left Wellington she came and sat by me and explained that she had arranged for all the passengers to come and sit by me in turn, so they could hear about England, London and the Queen. I was absolutely horrified and said, 'No way.' She was annoyed; so I explained that I was on a lecture workshop tour, the coach was very noisy, my voice must be rested on my one off day between engagements. With very bad grace she cancelled the 'all-change' seating arrangements and said she would go round and collect

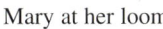

Mary at her loom

'Winter' - red silk kaftan

'Spring' - kaftan

'River Otter' - water-colour

Teaching at a workshop

Mary at Buckingham Palace with her nephew Christopher

Detail 'Autumn' from
'Four Seasons' kaftan

Detail 'Winter' from
'Four Seasons' kaftan

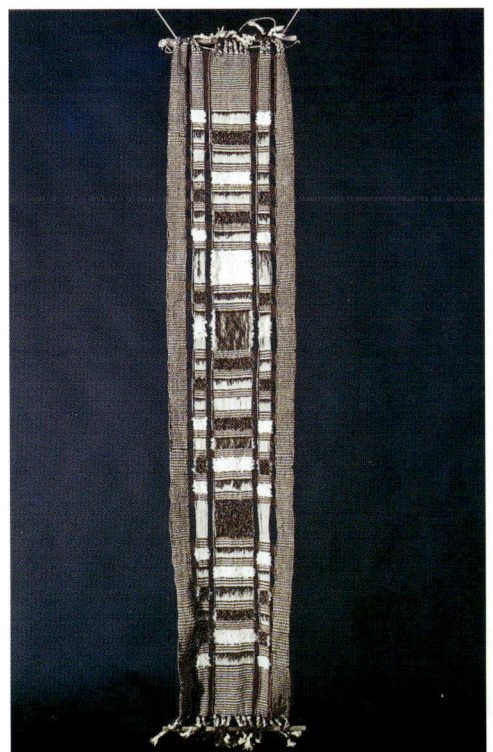

Hippy waistcoat to wear at workshops

Double cloth hanging

Sheila in yellow silk robe

Retrospective Exhibition, Lewes Town Hall, 1987

Wall-hanging sold to buyer in New Zealand

Silver feathered moon woven for New Zealand

'Sirens' - wall hanging

'Butterflies' - embroidery

people's questions and relay my answers. What with serving passengers their drinks, this programme was delayed for a while, and before she could really get going she had a serious problem on her hands. An outsized passenger had got wedged into a very small loo! Meanwhile, we got to the west coast, and I viewed in peace the island where the local Maoris had traditionally buried their chiefs. In warring with the white settlers the current chief was captured and imprisoned. He died in captivity and one night his warriors broke into the prison, recovered his body, and took him to be buried on the island. The Governor wisely turned a blind eye. I liked this legend and looked forward to meeting Maoris.

Strange facts float into my mind about Hamilton. First the Danish bungalow designed by its architect owners was my home for the week. Wooden furniture and fittings, shining wood floor, plenty of light, richly coloured curtains with abstract pattern and an absence of clutter made this a truly satisfying place. Second, I enjoyed the Danish food so much that I decided it would be good to have a walk to work one morning – only about a mile. Later I found the car that was to have given me a lift followed my progress at a discreet distance. Third memory was meeting a home-made loom that nearly defeated my efforts to make it work. Considering that many such constructions made during the war had fetched up in the weaving studios of Brighton College of Art and had been made to work quite easily, this was a challenge.

Next step was Auckland. Here the workshops and lecture went well. I met some talented weavers, potters, and loom builders and felt very much at home. People kept telling me how like England New Zealand was, but I found it very different. However, downtown Auckland was beginning to be a shadow of the swinging sixties of London town. One was never far from a sight of the sea, inlets on all sides dividing up the different districts. The Memorial Museum, standing on the top of the hill, was very impressive. Next visit I was to have an exhibition there as well as rooms to hold the workshops.

It was a hassle catching the plane for Christchurch, South Island, my next port of call. They held up the flight, rushed me across the tarmac, and wouldn't wait for my suitcase, saying it would follow, next journey. This was alarming as my lecture notes and party dress were needed for a performance that evening. However, I forgot all worries as Auckland and its amazing coastline spread out below my flight.

Christchurch did seem more like home. The trees in the park along the river reminded me of Cambridge, and one of the shops showed some St Michael's dresses – Marks and Spencer's brand. My belongings had turned up in time, so I gave my talk suitably dressed and went to the party at Ida Lough's, the tapestry weaver. To me, her work was the best I saw in New Zealand, with perhaps Mona Hessing taking first place in Australia. I was staying in a small hotel, and at breakfast next morning a couple came across to my table to introduce themselves. Their name was Ashford, and they were makers of spinning wheels. They had seen my photo and an account of my lecture in the local paper. They were to demonstrate their wheels at a training college that morning, and wanted to kidnap me to go too. However, my workshop was scheduled so I had to refuse. The results of this workshop were very pleasing.

Meantime, Ida had become a friend. I was taken to see her loom, which was in her bedroom. She beat her weft with a silver dinner fork, and that weft was often carpet wool as she, like myself, had worked for a carpet firm. She drove me out to the airport at the end of the week because I was to fly to Manipouri to spend the weekend with a weaver in her lakeside house. It was a beautiful day, blue sky with white clouds, but Ida looked at it distrustfully. 'Have you any travel pills? You'd better take them.' Most unnecessary, I thought, but meekly obeyed.

It was a splendid flight for about an hour and I was sitting next to a friendly young man with an elaborate camera. We were flying low enough to see hills and mountains. I still have a slide of an enchanting blue lake which he obligingly took for me with my simple Kodak. Suddenly we landed in a field. The pilot said we could not go up to Mount Cook because of cloudy weather, so the people at the hotel there would be brought down to the plane. There was a ladder on wheels and a tin marked FUEL, so this seemed a quite usual stop. It was an hour's wait and became rather tedious. I began to worry about my connection but they said the next plane would wait.

124

Eventually we started up again and landed at a small town, Queenstown, which was on the shores of a wide lake. I was not allowed time for even a coffee but was hustled onto a small plane that was waiting. There was the pilot, a steward and about six other passengers. We didn't fly very high. The plane rocked violently and people began to be sick. Even the steward had to sit down and strap himself in. We were flying along a valley between hills when the pilot said the weather was closing in and he'd have to try another route. Our little wings were flapping like those of a butterfly, and as we turned I gazed, eye to eye, with sheep feeding on the hillside. A kindly American sitting the other side of the gangway said, 'You look pale enough to faint, you'd better have some pills.' I was too frightened to feel sick. I just hoped the journey would soon end. He turned out to be a medical man and knew my hosts-to-be. He produced pills from his case, took one himself to reassure me, and gave me half a tumbler of whisky to swallow my pill down. I felt grateful as everyone else was being too sick to bother. Perhaps it was whisky courage, but I began to perk up and enjoy the wild sky, clouds dashing about and shooting off sparkling silver curtains of rain garnished with hailstones. After what seemed hours of being tossed up and down, the lake appeared below as a steel mirror. We were coming down to another bare field. There were a few cars on the lane nearby and a group of people standing watching. However, most of the field was flooded, and the pilot went round three times before he dared risk landing. We were all praying for a swift release from our prison. The plane stopped in a flurry of spray and the water was above my knees when I got out, but thank goodness there were people waiting to collect me. Pam's surgeon husband prescribed a hot drink, a bath and bed before food and I slept for an hour or two.

Their weekend house was built on the shore of Lake Te Anau, and the next evening we rowed across in the dinghy to the other side where the trees came down to the water. It was a narrow beach with pebbles and a few rocks to climb over. We pushed through the undergrowth into the bush – not very far in because of the fear of getting lost. I had only had a brief glimpse of Australian bush as yet, but immediately saw the difference, first in colour, then in form. The greens were darker, the plants rich in foliage, the atmosphere damp and cool. The sun was setting as we rowed back. Red reflections lined the ripples caused by the oars and the surface of the lake turned from silver to dark pewter.

On the Sunday they drove me through the tunnel under the mountains to Milford Sound, picnicking on the way. We boarded the small steamer for a trip down the sound. The high cliffs were dramatic, with little beaches at their feet. They were tunnelled by dark caves. The seabirds were swooping round in hope of food and there was even a seal basking on the shore. One thought of sailors on Captain Cook's exploring trips resting in the sounds, rowing ashore to find some fresh food to combat scurvy, shooting seabirds, and fishing. My hosts had said that it would be best if I drove back to Invercargill with them next day. I changed my ticket and flew back to Christchurch by the direct route, not the scenic one I'd come on.

I had to catch the connecting evening flight to Sydney. There was a delay on this journey. My New Zealand air trips were always adventurous. We didn't arrive back at the airport until so late the last bus had left for Sydney. There were a few passengers standing miserably around because no one had turned up to meet them. I discovered a girl who lived the other side of the harbour, like myself, so we shared an expensive taxi. My little hotel had shut up for the night. The owners did not live in the hotel but in a flat nearby and I was knocking at the door when another resident turned up, luckily with a pass key. So he let me in, we found an empty room and I settled in for that night.

Workshops in New Zealand had gone reasonably well, perhaps a little slower than those at home. They had needed more help and encouragement but results were satisfactory, so I was not worried when crossing the harbour in a day or so for the first Australian engagement. This was held at the Embroiderers' Guild, a couple of studios on the top of an eight-floor building looking out over a park. It was an extremely hot day and some of the pupils, led by an elderly teacher, did not take to the idea of traditional drafts used in a way the recipe book did not say. The idea of swapping looms horrified them. Worse, they had made mistakes in threading. Not much headway had been achieved by

126

lunchtime and I was wilting in the heat. Something must be done. So I swallowed my food and drink at top speed and had a go on the warp that looked most promising. Luckily it was a winner and the bright ones were eager to follow my example. Australians are dashing and direct. I soon found that instead of going round suggesting and praising it was a case of, 'Hi, half a moment – stop. Have you thought how it works on the back? Will it hold together when we cut it off the loom?' To my relief, by about three o'clock the elderly one was collapsing. We laid her on a sofa in the back room and phoned for her son to take her home. I was now getting results and everyone was eager to swap to the loom with the most exciting sample. Now it was, 'You must weave enough in the same way for your sample to be judged, otherwise when we cut them all up it won't be big enough to be valued.'

A few days later, my lecture to the Guild went surprisingly well. More workshops were planned, further afield in Melbourne, Canberra and even up in Queensland, besides some further engagements in Sydney. I decided that travel in Australia would be by train whenever possible. The scenery was entrancing. I did not want to miss any chance of seeing everything I could of this varied countryside, and it was only November 1970 when I returned to Australia after the New Zealand tour.

My tour of New Zealand had been hectic; my return passage to England was booked on the SS *Oronsay*, but she wasn't sailing until February so there was time to explore Sydney more leisurely and make new friends. New Zealand was already planning another visit for me in 1972, aided this time by a Queen Elizabeth II Craft Council grant.

Sydney became my home town. The Guild secretary, Eve Rashleigh, befriended me and everyone was very hospitable. It was a complete change from home and it was surprisingly easy to settle into this new life. People here, as in New Zealand, kept open house. It was like England in my childhood. My grandmother, with her large family, could always make room for one or two more, and at home, visitors for Father's Research Station were always being entertained. It seemed that in the colonies they had welcomed travellers from the early days on, and still kept up this habit. People I stayed with on my tours were all so kind to

127

me, showing the sights on my free days, and I never felt home-sick at all. It was always good to be billeted on a family where there were small children. The atmosphere there was very relaxed and there was plenty of opportunity to do one's washing and mending and get straight again.

Sometimes my daily programme was very tight. I was woken, say at 7, off at 8 for journeys across country to reach the site of the workshop – 8.45 for 9.00; 12.30 to 1.30 would be packed lunch or coffee time and we would finish around 3.45. At 4.20 one would arrive back at the billet, bedrest for me, chores for my hostess, who had also had a tiring day as a pupil. She now had to give the children supper, shoo them off to bath and bed, finish cooking for the dinner party, dress herself in glad rags then wake me. Possibly six or eight people would sit round her beautifully laid and flower-decorated table for a delicious meal, ending, of course, with a Pavlova. Then an extra mob would arrive for coffee and it was my turn to 'sing for my supper' with a slide show, extracted from one of my lectures. However quick I tried to be, allowing for questions after my chat, it was always about midnight before getting to my bed.

Back in Sydney there was time for me to explore. A perch on the rocks overlooking the harbour was a favourite place to sketch. It was called Lady McQuarrie's seat – she had been the wife of the first Governor. I sometimes thought that she must have watched, rather wistfully, the ships sailing back again to England. The Blue Mountains fascinated me. That would be a wonderful place to sketch but I never had time to paint a watercolour there. I visited Toronga Zoo, where all the giraffes were fascinating to watch, and I took a delightful slide of a young keeper feeding two baby kangaroos with bottles. I sampled bathing at Palm Beach and Bondi. Coming back from there one day, just before I sailed for home, the bus route passed a road away from the cricket ground. There was noisy roaring and shouting, almost like baying of hounds. I asked the driver what it was. He said, 'I guess Boycott's on his way to another century and annoying the crowd.' A month or so later, on the liner making for home, we had a celebration because the British had won the test match series that year – February 1971.

One day, on a visit to the centre of the city, I witnessed a touching sight. The traffic stopped on a main road cleared from cars, spectators lined the pavements, a small party of soldiers marched to a spot and formed up, a gun fired and all was silent. After a minute the Last Post was sounded. Men replaced their hats and traffic moved again. That evening at dinner in my small hotel I mentioned this to the proprietor, and asked what ceremony this was. The whole room listened. He said, 'Remembrance for the war, of course. Don't you have similar parades in Britain?' I replied, 'Yes, but it isn't November the eleventh.' Everyone looked puzzled. The host said, 'We have them every week – don't you?' 'No,' was my reply. They took this as very wrong, so I thought very quickly how to save my country's reputation and explained that there were so many battles and wars to commemorate in Great Britain's history – Waterloo, Trafalgar, Agincourt, Crécy, the Battle of Hastings, etc. – there would not be enough time to commemorate them all!

That little hotel in Cremorne had been found for me by an English friend who had settled in Australia. It was a good place in which to find one's feet in a new country. There were several young people who had just arrived in Australia, staying there. They were busy finding a job, making friends and then they moved off into flats or houses. We used to congregate in the lounge, laughing about the mistakes we made in getting acclimatised. The proprietor acted as waiter in the dining room, where there were separate tables, but in his easy Italian manner he orchestrated general conversation between Australians and us migrants. Half board was a cooked breakfast and a generous filling three-course meal at 6 p.m. too early in the evening for me. There were numerous juice bars in Sydney for light lunches and I absolutely fell for apricot juice. Tinned or bottled, the apricot never tastes like the real thing.

My digestion was suffering from overfeeding; Australians have very hearty appetites, so on my return to Sydney I took a flatlet opposite the hotel and at once felt better on my own usual light diet. Another reason for this move was that all my frequent comings and goings from the hotel meant that each time I came back from a journey, a different room was allocated to me. This was unsettling and the flatlet gave me an opportunity to grow a few Australian roots. Permanent jobs were offered to me and the decision would have to be made. Pros and cons would have to be studied carefully. In actual fact instinct provided the right answer. I was in the back of a fast car being driven on a journey from Melbourne down the Prince's Highway. The driver turned round to me and asked, 'Why don't you take this particular offer?' No other car was in sight, but our speed was between 70 and 80 miles per hour and most Aussie accidents seem to be one car just going off the road and hitting a tree, so a quick answer was essential. 'Too far from London,' was my reply, and if I had worried for days I don't think I could have made a more true decision.

Because not all Guilds with members have looms and weave, details of workshops, drafts, methods of cloth structure, etc. will be given in an appendix. However, there was one ambitious project organised by Sydney Guild that might be of interest for other disciplines. They had a dyeing weekend specialising in their local plants, particularly garden varieties, and also on another occasion a spinning one. They asked me if I could plan a workshop for around 40 weavers to take place during a long weekend at a country craft centre in the bush, which was let out for such purposes. The students would be of mixed ability and would bring their own looms already set up to particulars that would be given to them in advance. My plan was to have a variety of space warps, all white. Ten in four groups, ranging from simple rigid heddle and two-shaft looms up to an eight-shaft loom. We all assembled and it was a beautiful place. Before dinner that night they took me for a walk down to the creek where there was a peculiar net arrangement hung, about 50 yards from the head of this waterway, and I asked them what this was. They said, 'This stream goes out to the sea eventually so we have a shark net, but it is possible to bathe this side of the net.' I didn't really fancy that. The variety of gum trees surrounding the little terraced veranda all round the building, mostly in wood, made a delightful setting for the craft centre. We had a delicious dinner and I explained what they were going to do the following day. Then several people had to finish threading up their warps.

Their first sample was to be woven in white, in plain weave, using one of the warp yarns as weft. I wanted them to weave for one hour, possibly completing the 6-inch sample. I had left the width to individuals as it did depend on how many heddles their loom had, but the ends per inch varied from 12 to 48. At the end of an hour we did a tour of the looms, appraising what had been done. Most failures were the wrong choice of the size of weft yarn or else the weft had not been beaten in firmly enough. So I persuaded everyone to try a second sample from their own warp. After a second criticism and discussion, it was time to suggest different ways of grouping threads together, using the spaces, finger gauze, Spanish lace, Brooks bouquet etc. Some people in their own group were ready to swap looms, some of the warps being used up rapidly. Indeed, we had to wind some more warps and rethread that evening. Each section had had at least three variations of yarn and spacing. After a slow start and some quibbling about using plain weave, everybody was getting enthusiastic. The second day, I asked them to design something specific – curtain material, place mats, vision blinds or even dress material. Now colour, different weaves were allowed – no holds barred – anything you could think of. This was an experiment for me. I had never tried this before, but exploring one cloth construction in depth brought some splendid results. However, the really best samples were all white in plain weave and really very simple variations of the warp. The display at the end of Sunday afternoon was quite impressive, and everyone felt very pleased with what they had achieved. We had a celebration dinner. Indeed, it went on so long that someone had to rush me back to Sydney to catch the night sleeper train in a hurry. And due to Sunday evening traffic on the main highway, we just rushed onto the platform for me to leap into the last carriage.

I enjoyed travelling with a sleeper compartment. I always asked to be called early with my breakfast and let up the venetian blind to look through at the countryside slipping past. Birds and animals were so used to the train passing at a certain time that it did not seem to disturb them much. Flocks of their grey parrots, called galahs, used to spring up and swing into the sky in a lovely circular movement, and as they did so you saw the rosy colour under their wings and bodies. It was a glorious sight.

Also kangaroos quite happily hopped near the line, behaving just naturally. The train obviously was a normal feature of their lives.

The day got hotter and hotter, and when at last I arrived at Adelaide I was being paged, 'Mary Barker, Mary Barker', on the tannoy. A Guild member had come to meet me and rushed up saying, 'The television people want you. They are waiting. They are holding the programme, so we've got to go to the studio at once.'

I said indignantly, 'I'm hot, tired and dirty from the train journey. I must at least wash and change into a fresh dress before I appear on television.' I had never done this before. They seemed to think it was a good idea and promised to have something else before it was my turn. So I was rushed to someone's home, got a clean dress hastily out of my suitcase, popped it on, washed my face, did my hair and was dashed to the studio just as everyone was getting anxious.

There wasn't time to rehearse me. They made me up while the producer said, 'Watch me and I shall signal to you how it is going.' So with that I was shoved on.

The interviewer was a very smart piece of work. I took against her from the start. She said something very superior, lacking knowledge about weaving and so, politely, I said, 'Oh no – that isn't right.' So my friend the producer waved to me encouragingly out of sight of the camera. I put her straight and this really continued throughout the interview. She was getting a little bit irritated with me by the time we finished. But I simply had been so rushed and was so tired after the weekend and the long journey that I did not care what she felt or thought.

When we finished, I spoke anxiously to the producer, 'I'm sorry, I was a little annoyed that she hadn't done any homework, she didn't seem to know anything about it. She didn't really ask me the right questions.'

He said, 'Oh that's all right, you made a very spirited interviewee,' and with that I had to be content.

The Guild then rushed me out to where the workshop was to be held, and I must say that I do not think they got full value out of their first day. However, we got started and I was still there when the interview was shown on television. It must have been

132

quite successful because it got reported in the newspaper with a photo of myself, and when I came to give the lecture, which was in the small theatre, we had a full house.

The evening before my lecture, I was resting on my bed when an insistent visitor arrived. My hostess was saying that she could not disturb me when I suddenly recognized a voice from my past, and called, 'Come in!' It was Joyce, one of our Third Officer WRNS at Cardiff. We had not met since 1945 and this was 26 years later. She roared with laughter to see me spending time off lying flat out. It was a familiar sight. After D-Day, when I had worked myself to a standstill and had to have an operation, she had often seen me in the same position. Joyce had married, gone out and settled in Australia and had had two children, both grown up now, and even had a grandchild. We had so much to tell about various friends as well as about our own lives, it was a wonder I had any voice left for that lecture. Encounters like this make the world seem very small.

Adelaide was a city with a beautiful centre. The young officer in command had looked down on the site from a hill and decided to build a city on a square formation, bisected with cross-roads, with wide avenues all round the centre square. He named it after King William IV's consort, Adelaide. The houses in the centre reflect the architecture of that pre-Victorian era. There is a beautiful botanical garden with a fantastic glass conservatory.

When there was no time to do a sketch, slides were taken as reminders. But somehow they are not so evocative as a few scribbled lines of one's own. Someone drove me out through the vineyards (Adelaide produces delicious wines) and up a mountain, so that we looked down on the city.

The house there was an art and craft museum and it was very, very hot that day. I was not very impressed with the exhibits so I wandered off to explore the gardens and found an untidy greenhouse, and some roughcast bricks with names, dates or marks carved into their surface. These spoke of homesickness to me, and the curator was pleased with me for finding them. He said such convict bricks, relics of the past, were becoming collector's pieces as people became proud of their ancestry. Even

150 years later one could feel the nostalgia of these early settlers. Both Paddington and The Rocks in Sydney show how their memories of Regency architecture became overexaggerated, so they built balconies with delicate lace-like ironwork rather more elaborate than we have at home. I actually stayed in Camberwell, a district in Melbourne, in a bungalow that was a typical ground floor of an early Victorian mansion, double-fronted windows and rooms with heavy cornices round the ceiling.

Travelling through parts of the countryside, one would see a group of trees sheltering a farmhouse and outbuildings in the distance, very reminiscent of parts of the country over here. A nearer view might be a let-down because they would have a corrugated iron roof and the trees are not the sort of trees we have here at home. The early settlers' lives, and those of the Aborigines, interested me wherever travel took me. The native myths and legends were a source of rich enjoyment. I visited museums wherever possible to sketch Aboriginal relics.

Looking back all these years later, place names bring to mind vivid pictures. Melbourne for that splendid museum with water trickling continuously down the whole glass front – very cool on a hot day. There was one particular gallery where statues of Khan Yin were kept and which could be seen through a small garden enclosure with tall slender trees growing out of the gravel, shivering gently in the wind. Another memory during my stay was when an English family took me on a picnic to the Dandelongs, where they said you could watch for the lyre-birds. I could hear them calling but never saw one. They are very shy. Canberra, like Adelaide, had a dramatic layout when seen from above with the Snowy Mountains surrounding it. My best memory, however, besides that bush fire described earlier, was finding some splendid hard seed pods under a tree in the university garden. Just what was needed to weight a 3-D wall hanging we were busy constructing.

I had been a little concerned about the heat on my first visit to Brisbane, but need not have worried. There had been no rain there for some years. On my day off, a picnic was arranged to show off their rainforests. We were eating lunch in a clearing by the side of the road, and English fashion, I looked at the cloudy sky and feared a downpour. My host laughed at me and said, 'Some hope. It hasn't rained here since goodness knows when – at least seven years or so.' We continued up the mountain and walked through the rainforests – very impressive tall trees but dark and rather eerie. Great clouds were looming and the day was darkening and I was sure it was going to rain. And it did! We got back to the car soaked through. After that I earned the nickname of 'bringer of rain'. Rain often happened wherever I went, not just drizzle but silver splashing fountains, taps turned full on, flooding and soaking everything round about. I remember once in Cremorne walking downhill to the ferry when the raindrops hit the ground so hard they splashed up to my waist, and I was wet through, bottom as well as head and shoulders. Luckily, in the heat, one dries off quickly.

One cherished memory was of a visit to a small settlement north of Perth. We stayed in a wooden settler's cottage, living much as the settlers would have done. There was a tall, pink pepper tree, much taller than the roof, beside it. All water was pumped up in primitive fashion. The settlement was surrounded by hills and the story goes that when they were first building there, the Aborigines would gather on the heights to watch. They were particularly interested in the men with 'sticks that spoke fire' and could kill animals and birds. All was peaceful until one of their men was wounded. Then they came down at night and burned the huts down.

The situation in Australia had changed by my second visit. The price of their wool sales had dropped dramatically, so sheep farmers were feeling unusual poverty. Their womenfolk turned to weaving, spinning and knitting in the hope of selling these items for a little money. The tourist trade was increasing, with the result that small galleries or craft shops were opening up and were needing merchandise to sell. Everyone was to supply suitable goods to attract visitors. Sadly, a great deal of work produced was of low quality. Owners of galleries needed help in judging what to promote. Everywhere I went, the Guild Committee would ask that I should vet the local craft shop and offer advice to the proprietor. It soon was obvious that I must shed my escort and be alone with the owner. Then it was easy to speak freely, point out

135

the faults bluntly and leave them with a checklist of what to look for. They knew their market and had an eye for anything unusual. Mostly they seemed very quick as students.

This visit I concentrated on two types of workshop. New Zealand had asked for a week's programme, perhaps leading to an examination equivalent to our City and Guilds Handweaving Certificate. They felt some standards should be set as the textile crafts were becoming popular. I spent most of the week on the usual syllabus but I included a design day, using foundation year exercises, as done in art schools, to demonstrate the first principles of design. Each exercise was done in similar dimensions, and at the end of the day everyone's effort was mounted on sepia paper and the results were often astonishingly good. The other workshop would be for three days in places where I was making a long enough stay to have an interval between each session. For instance, I gave a general title – Adventures in Interlacement. This seemed to appeal to Australians. The subjects were wall hangings or 3-D constructions. They were really intended for the more skilled craftsman. For Day 1, I would demonstrate and give an introduction so that people could have an idea how to plan their project. We then would discuss all problems, make a list for each student of all the requirements and explain how to start, and they would then go away and work on their idea. On Day 2, they would bring what they had done, problems would have to be settled, suggestions made and errors corrected. Another week would be spent on their work and on Day 3, we decided how to finish and display each wall hanging. It was a proud moment when we viewed the final exhibition.

11

Second Overseas Tour – 1972:
Australia, New Zealand, USA and Canada

The English countryside looked at its delicate best – pale soft greens, primroses, yellow daffodils and early pink and white blossoming trees. I was so proud and delighted that my New Zealand and Australian friends on board would see that the sun could shine in rainswept Britain.

The Mead - Long Ashton

This first homecoming was a sad one. Father's house at Long Ashton, The Mead, was to be emptied and sold by auction. I had known this house since early childhood. The family who lived there were a little older than the boys and myself but we had often been to parties, and even a dance there. At one stage it had been a boys' prep school and the story goes that the writer Beverley Nichols once called there to see his old school. One entered from the main road into a yard with a stable block one side and a pathway led through a flower garden, sheltered by an apple tree in front of the third cottage, to reach the new front door that Father had made. He had closed the dangerous entry the other side of the house from the main road, and shut up that front door when he bought The Mead, and had even put in a different new staircase. The room upstairs had been of the communal sort that you walk through one to get to another, but Father put in new walls to make each bedroom self-contained.

The house really consisted of three cottages and a barn which had been joined together by a connecting two-storey wing some centuries ago. There was a giant magnolia growing up the former barn wall, framing French doors which led to the upper garden from the lounge. This garden was enclosed by the L-shape of the house. On the south side was a terrace and steps down to a tennis court. In the sunny corner between cottages one and two, Father had built a greenhouse. The fruit and vegetable garden was screened by espalier apple trees one side and a herbaceous border the other. A stepping stone path led up to the lawn and in winter this was lined by a lovely blue blaze of iris stylosa. My nephew Christopher, as a tiny boy, had once brought one or two down from his home as a present for Alicia, who was my stepmama, which had now spread along the path.

By the lawn, a yucca, after being blown over in the storm, had rooted all along its thick stem and then several creamy flower spikes had grown instead of just one. It was quite spectacular. Stepmama sold off most of this garden and a modern house had been built there, which spoilt the property, so it was sold for only about £11,000 at auction. This money was put in a trust fund for Shirley, my half-sister, and myself, to share the income. I felt this unfair to my brothers and sisters and protested to Stepmama when she told me what she had put in her will, but she was adamant. Her reason was that I was the only one who had treated the house as home and looked after Father in my holidays so that she could go away with my half-sister. The fact that I enjoyed being there with him was immaterial.

About 15 years later the next owners sold the house for £100,000. There was a wonderful view, down over the valley to a stream and then gently rising hills eventually to Dundry, where adding on the height of the church tower, a square early Norman one, made Dundry as tall as a mountain. As children we loved that stream. We played boat races with twigs and fell into it and generally messed about, as children will. Sadly, soon after Father died the fields below us were sold for development. Now the poor old Mead can hardly be seen from down below; the field is filled up with a housing development, which they have christened Ashton Thuynes, an ancient name. Father used to lie in bed and look out of the window and see the railway line far enough away to be like a toy, and he named the train his getting-up train – he watched it when he was older, as a signal for when he should get up. A bypass, also, was constructed which ran through the scenery. When it is distant enough a bypass can be quite an elegant addition to the view. We were all so glad that this development did not take place in Father's time.

Another sadness was that I was back just in time to go to Mary Bryan's farewell party at college. Her operation the previous summer had not been the hoped-for success. She died the following Easter. My own house had not suffered during my absence. My nice help, Mrs Ottaway, kept it clean and aired, and my adopted cousin Sylvia collected the rents. As soon as definite news of the New Zealand grant came through, I began planning my journey. This time I was taking out an exhibition of work, so again was to travel by sea. Incredible as it seems now, the return trip, first-class on the *Oriana*, was cheaper than my original round world ticket on the SS *Arcadia* and SS *Oronsay*, tourist class. Again, I was circling the world, but this time it would be straight across the Pacific, just calling at Fiji, Samoa and Hawaii, then Vancouver, San Francisco, Los Angeles and Acapulco.

Several places had invited me to bring an exhibition of my

work with me. This was shown in New Zealand, at the Museum and Art Gallery in Christchurch, at the Memorial Museum in Auckland, and at the Old Post Office in Dunedin; also in Australia at craft shops and galleries in Sydney, Melbourne, Canberra, Brisbane and Perth. I did sell most of my wall hangings before sailing for home, which perhaps was a mistake; one should keep some of one's best work as a record. It was an honour to be shown at Christchurch because it was the first time they had included crafts exhibitions.

In Dunedin, I had another experience of appearing on television. This time it was a planned effort. The Old Post Office was a solid stone building with a lovely polished floor and a little platform, a fine hall for showing textiles. The Guild had displayed my handiwork very well and there were great big jars filled with exotic leaves and flowers which further decorated the scene. A producer came to see us at work, upstairs where we had the looms, and decided that several of the looms should be brought down into the gallery and that the interviewer should sometimes talk to me; they would sometimes take shots of people actually at work, with me bending over teaching them, and then the interviewer and I would walk round looking at some of the wall hangings they picked out, talking about each one in turn. All seemed to be going well, but when they brought the interviewer to see me first and he was saying what he was going to ask and telling me what to answer him, I did not care for the man very much. He didn't seem to know much about weaving and I thought his comments were superficial and silly, much as I had done on the earlier occasion in Adelaide in Australia. However, they proceeded with what they thought was their programme and all went well until he was having a little chat with me about weaving before going round the hangings.

Again I put him right when he was wrong. This I did in quite a spirited fashion so he wasn't very pleased with me when we were looking at the hangings. But all in all, it made for quite a good programme. We all watched it excitedly an evening or two later on TV. The only thing that marred it a little was that one of their best-known weavers was working on a very simple heddle loom. This amused the New Zealanders very much.

There was quite a lot of publicity with the exhibitions. I remember in Perth an interviewer came again to see me to get the usual photographs and story, and it turned out that although we were getting the publicity it was that he had noted my English address and that he had been born and brought up at No. 7 Harrington Road, so he wanted to talk about his old home. It was a strange coincidence so far from Brighton. For this visit, the programme was far more structured. New Zealand had asked for a weekly programme, roughly based on the City and Guilds syllabus, for their special hand weaving exam which C & G had put on for the Weavers' Guild in England. I was used to this as my part-time students frequently took it. We had hoped that this, together with the advanced hand weaving exam, would lead to a teacher's certificate as in the case of City and Guilds Embroidery, but sadly the numbers of weavers taking this did not warrant the expense and it was discontinued. In my view, City and Guilds, the guardians of standards of craftmanship, was sadly needed in the rapid increase of weavers who had little opportunity of attending professional classes. I regretted their decision to stop this test.

The Association of Guilds of Weavers, Spinners and Dyers many years later set up their own Certificate of Achievement. I was one of the examiners for this for the first few years. The crafts of weaving, spinning and dyeing were taken as separate disciplines, and although the candidates had studied their chosen subject in some depth, they were tending to lack the satisfactory cohesion that the old City and Guilds certificate gave.

Returning to my tour, detailed notes on the planned week will be given in the Appendix. I had sent out a required reading list and also the warp plans, as before, asking that the students should bring some of their handspun, vegetable-dyed wool for use. Day 3 was to be a design day, a mini version of some of the exercises set for foundation course art students. This was an attempt to show the value of useful traditional design balance, contrast, space relationships, etc. There were five exercises, all to be done on the same size sheets of paper with coloured pencils, chalks or paints, according to the choice of the student, and all were mounted, when finished, on sepia brown paper so we could have a criticism at the end of the day when they were put up on the boards. By looking at them for the rest of the week some of the principles might be absorbed unconsciously. If anyone found it too difficult, I cheated and lent a helping hand so everyone was quite happy about what they had on display. We did the usual swapping round of looms, once the orthodox samples had been woven. I was strict about weaving particulars being accurately noted and also size of samples. Everything was cut off the looms by lunchtime on the last day so they could be textile wet finished. Most people went home with a useful portfolio of samples for both dress and furnishing materials. My hope was that these would lay the foundations of fabrics of super weight and draping qualities for their purpose. I had noticed this was often sadly lacking.

When I was going to stay longer in the same city, such as Sydney or Melbourne, I planned a different type of workshop for adventurous weavers who wanted to branch out and make wall hangings or 3-D constructions. On the first day we sorted out individuals' ideas, did a rough sketch of the design, decided on yarns, colours, size and method – a day of extremely hard work for myself, keeping everybody occupied. They all wanted individual help to get started. They then went home and worked on their project. The following week they came to class, bringing their hanging to check that all was well. Sometimes it wasn't, but in the general critical atmosphere we all learned a great deal. There were plenty of suggestions and it was interesting for me to see how people had interpreted their basic sketch. Sometimes we had to unpick a section, add a new element of shape, colour and texture, but by the end of that second day there was hope of some exciting finished work being brought in on Day 3. Someone trying for an advertising title, christened this type of workshop as 'Adventures in Interlacement'. Although from the first sketch, plans had been made about how the work was to hang, there was plenty of consideration to be made about getting the right finish; binding a cord; what about macramé, to fringe or hem, and with 3-D the method of suspension and finding a suitable weight. The variety was amazing, and after the first trial round, dyeing was introduced and a range of colour light, medium, dark to give tapestry-like constructions a subtlety and softness. I was always on the lookout for unusual weights and was absolutely delighted when, after lunch at Canberra University staff restaurant, we were walking across the lawns under a tree with marvellous, hard almost wooden seed pods. We picked up several of these to act as weights when needed.

At last it was time to go home. On the way out, SS *Oriana* had been in trouble. We weren't very far out from Southampton before we had to spend time in our life jackets in the lounge because of a fire alarm. Other things too went wrong on the voyage. Now, when it was time for the homeward trip, I was ready and boarded the ship quite happily, never realising this time it was my farewell to Australia and New Zealand. I had felt very much at home out there and loved making a temporary home at Cremorne.

Jobs for a year or so had been offered to me but, somehow, I felt I needed to establish some pattern of life in retirement. I had not yet had time to make up my mind whether to sell my house in Brighton and go back to the West Country to be near the family. This would mean giving up the *Weavers' Journal* and my pad at 119 Hornsey Lane. All my London life and countless friends there would be difficult to keep in touch with. Life, first-class on a luxury liner, was no place to make decisions. Perhaps it was not quite so lively as tourist travel had been the first trip but again there were plenty of friends to share all the pleasures of travel, visits ashore, my morning bathe, keep-fit class, delicious food, new films and new books. Then there was the everlasting sea's endless variations. It changed every hour, almost every minute, my eyes could never tire of looking at the entrancing blueness. There was drama in sky changes and reflection, different colour schemes for dawn, midday and dusk. Memories of this have influenced my design ever after.

I got back to my house to find the hotel, which was attached to me on both sides, had been sold. Longley's, the large building firm centred at Crawley, had bought it. My friends Nan and Jack Barnes, who had started the hotel, had moved into my garden flat when the students left at the end of the summer term. They planned to use it as a base, while travelling abroad most of the time, but as it happened they were at home most of the year. It was a very happy household until they left on the ill-fated journey by car across France to Menton, where Jack died suddenly. Nan stayed on, making it her home, with the two cats, Top Cat and Twiggy, for the next five years. We used to go to Brighton's Theatre Royal every week, no matter what was on, for the equivalent, at first, of two bob, in the gallery. We had our regular seats up there. Nan was a wizard at parking her yellow MG Spitfire even in crowded Brighton and we rushed around all over Sussex.

I still kept up my London life and made no real decision to go west. In 1974 there was to be a World Craft Conference in Toronto. I had wanderlust again and began to plan another tour based around this. It was only to last around three months because my youngest niece was getting married in the summer and I wanted to be back for her wedding. The liner *QEII* was making regular sailings to New York, so why not travel by sea again? The French liner SS *France* was sailing back at the right date. This time both passages were booked successfully. Southampton never seemed to be a lucky port for me, and on this voyage travellers had to say farewell in a shore lounge. We were then whisked out of sight of friends and relatives, divided into male and female queues and given a thorough sailors' strip search before being allowed on board. This was because there had been troubles on *QEII*, threats of sabotage, etc.

My berth was to be a single bed, in a cabin for three. The two other occupants had top and bottom berths. When I got down to the cabin an elderly uncouth Irish woman was sitting firmly on my bed and refused to give it up; worse still, she had a long narrow wooden box roped carefully up which she stored beneath that bed. After the search alarmist thoughts of gun-running flashed through my mind but there was nothing much that could be done, so I went up to dinner. On my return I found the third occupant had turned up and was weeping on my berth. Old Mrs Irish was shouting at the poor young girl and both were getting hysterical. I couldn't comfort her and and went off to find a friendly steward. He said it was too late that night to do anything, but first thing next morning I was to go to the bureau and ask for a transfer. He would report to the purser.

I returned to my berth and in best paymaster fashion told my companions to shut up or there would be trouble. The girl and myself spent an uneasy night listening to Irish snores and snorts.

Next morning the purser took the key to a first-class cabin in the bows and said that it was to be mine, with no extra charge, if I liked. They moved my gear promptly and from then on I had the free run of the whole ship. A quick decision was made to breakfast in bed, lunch and dine in tourist, where I had already made friends at my table, and swim, have afternoon tea and late night drinks in first class, attending evening entertainment in either which appealed to me best. Afternoons I spent in a financial seminar with a cluster of millionaires, first class. There was just one other woman there and when the spry, whizz kid lecturer asked questions of his audience, she and myself were the only ones who answered him. My Stock Exchange plan was then in an early growth situation, but I really learned valuable lessons about investing that I have remembered to this day. Our companions woke up when the delicious tea was served and were suitably gallant. Often I wondered how their wealth was acquired – perhaps, by now, they were worn out by their successful efforts. The indoor swimming pool was a delight. Luxury again, individual changing cabins with free powders and lotions, masses of soft bath towels, a bar and plenty of lounging chairs round the pool. This was rather small, but deep. As the other occupants either sat on stools at the bar or lay around on the loungers in the latest swimwear, I needn't have worried about its size. I usually had the pool to myself. The tourist pool on deck was much bigger but always crowded.

Having already sailed into, or departed from, some of the most beautiful harbours in the world, I was rather disappointed in New York. True, the skyscrapers shone, misty silvery pink on the skyline, but the Statue of Liberty looked surprisingly dumpy and middle-aged as we passed her. Disembarking was swift. An ex-student, who had experienced the difficulties of small cheap hotels there (I did not want the grand ones), had advised me to try the YMCAs while I found my way around. The London headquarters had provided a list and booked me a room in a central skyscraper mixed YM and YWCA. It was not a long taxi ride, but on arrival I found the YW part was segregated on the 16th floor, cut off from the rest of the establishment. The cafeteria was on the ground floor, noisy and crowded and I didn't like the food there. I don't really like heights and the lift up and down was not a happy experience. I stayed there the first night, went out for meals, walked around, found the Museum of Modern Art and Fifth Avenue. The next day I discovered another YW, better situated, which had been the Sherlock Holmes Hotel. They had a room with bath for me, a nice view over the harbour, and would also store my spare suitcases for me whenever I went away for short visits. The food was delicious.

My new home actually had a craft centre on the second floor and there was a weaving class in session. I went down to see them and received an enthusiastic welcome. They did not belong to the American Weaver's Guild, which had branches all over the country, so could tell me nothing about the Guilds I was visiting. There were two or three days spare before my first engagement so there was time to explore New York properly. Excursions were excellent. There was a trip round the harbour. In between outings, I explored museums, Central Park, and of course, the shops along Fifth Avenue. It was surprisingly economical living my way. I lunched at cafeterias, but found it easy to have coffee and rests at the good hotels and stores. People of all colours and races were friendly and direct. Australians had also been very open and straightforward in much the same manner as Yorkshire folk were when I first went up to Leeds University. New Yorkers were different; they seemed to go out of their way to help and instruct me. This was a surprise. I have always been independent and able to find my own way.

My first lecture was to be at Hertford, north of New York. It was back to feeling like a parcel waiting for delivery when arriving at the station. My hosts, the Guild secretary and her young husband, were a delightful couple. I felt at ease at once in their home. They were off on a canoeing weekend, camping with friends, next day, and were busy packing for the expedition. By the time the Guild's special Open Meeting was over on the Saturday, they were trying to persuade me to join the camp and canoe trip. I would have loved to have gone but the editor of

146

Shuttle, Spindle and Dyepot had invited me for the weekend. We had had a friendly correspondence over our respective journals and there were several matters it was policy to discuss.

American Guilds certainly arrange their Open Days in fine style. A competition was to be judged and although I had brought a small exhibition as well as slides for my lecture, the Committee, a bit self-important in comparison with my easy-going hosts, kept interfering; didn't know if it was a good idea if my hangings were shown – would they upset the competition and competitors etc? Eventually they were shown behind the screens so they should not compete. Thank goodness for that concession; I sold one to the prizewinner at a handsome price. Lunch, and eventually tea, were absolutely delicious, laid out delightfully on long tables decorated with floral trophies. It reminded me a bit of Mothers' Union meetings long ago in the village hall. Among all the judging and the speeches and business, time for my lecture eroded. I managed a shortened version, going rapidly over some slides. It got a good reception, but privately I wondered if they had had their money's worth, because the fee was generous.

My weekend was spent in luxury – people talk about the glorious fall in New England but some of those trees that turn to brilliant reds in autumn were blossoming in delicious varied pinks and whites, set off by tender fresh new greens in spring. The guest room had a half-circle bath with a swan head tap and shower.

On Sunday morning my hosts were going on a picnic expedition to their fishing lodge on one of the lakes. Another couple were joining them. En route we stopped at a supermarket to stock up on provisions for the day. My host said, 'You come in and have a look, you haven't yet got anything like this at home.' And indeed it was an eye-opener. The fishing lodge was delightful, log cabin style, situated in this wood a few yards above the lake. We had a quick lunch and then the men got the boat launched and rowed out to fish. I got a bit bored and wandered off to explore the shore, regretting that I hadn't my sketchbook. I picked up a nicely grained pebble or two, a bird's feather and a few small pieces of weather-beaten wood. When I got back, they said, 'Just like Theo Moorman when she was here.' Eventually, fish was brought back and cooked for the evening meal. It was late when we got back. Early next morning I was to see the editor's office before being put on the Greyhound for Boston. The Weaver's Guild there were very good at taking me around but my visit did not coincide with their meeting date. After three days, it was back to New York.

It seemed silly not to have a visit to Washington when it was so near. So, instead of going straight to Chicago by plane, I went down by train to Washington for three days then travelled on the overnight train to Chicago. In Washington I stayed at another YW, beautifully furnished, as luxuriously as the Boston one had been. Their drawing room was Victorian but at home in a similar room many periods would have been included. I spoke to the Director about this and she said it was usual for one of the ladies on the committee when they died, or redecorated, to give unwanted furniture to the YWs. I had the fun of queuing for the White House with the public holiday crowd, who made much of an English stranger; visited the museums and art gallery, revelling in the marvellous Impressionists collection, and discovered for the first time how dangerous America could be. The YW was just round the corner from the Hilton Hotel and one evening I walked round to buy stamps. There was a crowd outside, and the police. There had been a murder. Apparently, two couples, visitors from the hotel, were just getting into a taxi when a man approached, asking for their wallets. They refused, he pulled a gun, shot one dead, wounded another and drove off in the taxi. After that I lugged my case by bus to the station.

The journey to Chicago went through wonderful unspoilt scenery, the reclining seats were really comfortable, and I slept well. Chicago was another example of dangerous America. After I was met at the station we went to park the car in an underground car park. There was a large notice saying, 'Alarm Bell. Ring for an escort before leaving your car.' It was a public holiday and the place was empty. My hostess said, 'There are often muggings here.' I felt almost more nervous of the armed escort than of the possible mugger. Presently we drove to the hospital where her husband was in charge. As we passed through one derelict district she told me that it had the 'black blight'. Gradually all white families were driven further out into the suburbs to live because of their children's education. Apparently teachers had to teach from wire cages because the unruly children would assault them and throw missiles. Several families then moved into a house built for a single family and discipline was impossible. I trust that this situation is better now. My engagement here as at Aubourn was for a Design Day. There were around 20 students, ranging from art students to 80-year-olds. The usual routine, in spite of my fears, went with a swing and the results made an impressive display in the elegant hall. For once my fee seemed well earned.

It was time to use my Greyhound bus pass to travel to Ottawa. I stayed overnight at Detroit at another YWCA. Travel this way was an excellent experience, not only for getting a close-up of the scenery but a chance to know all sorts of people. Everyone was kind and helpful to inexperienced me, quite different from travel at home. Another overnight stop was at Toronto, where I rang my god-daughter Shirley. We hadn't met for 20 years. Eventually I reached the Four Seasons Hotel in Ottawa, which was to be home to myself and an American potter called Ernie, who took a parallel week's course at the same college. Quite a shock to move from YWCAs to luxury. I had a suite – hall, bathroom, wardrobe, refrigerator, four beds in an enormous room with lounge chairs and an immense TV. Ernie had a similar suite. Meals were equally lavish. As our pupils were very hospitable we felt the organisers could have spent less on our accommodation, possibly more on the fees.

It was an enjoyable week for myself as well as the weavers. They seemed to be harder workers than the potters. The college was situated on the banks of a river, where weavers hastily gobbled their salad lunch to get back to their looms, leaving potters happily enjoying drinks in the sunshine. One day Ernie summoned my gang to a lecture. He had set up four slide projectors at once. The slides moved at various speeds. It was dazzling and was supposed to be stimulating. I peered round at my flock after the first half-hour. Some had shut their eyes, others had crept away, some were enjoying a nap. The varied image did suggest ideas to me but too long exposure just gave one a shattering headache.

Ottawa had many subjects for sketching and I was busy drawing and sightseeing in my time off. The International Crafts Conference at Toronto was enjoyable. The exhibitions were good, and plenty of workshops were arranged, which gave opportunities to chat to fellow craftsmen. There were happenings, discussions, mass meetings, impressive lectures, big formal parties and tiny gatherings of like-minded people. I came to the conclusion that this sort of conference really did little good. It was too vast compared with the aspirations of each country and each individual craftsman; all their wants were so different.

Craft seemed to be an umbrella word covering everything from tourist gifts to works of art. It was an expensive occasion both for government grants and individuals' pockets. Still, everyone seemed to be having an enjoyable time. On Sunday my goddaughter Shirley collected me for sightseeing round the city and home to meet her four children. Driving back at dusk to Toronto University I was terrified by a 16-lane highway on which you had to get into the right lane for your exit about three miles beforehand. Every vehicle was travelling at high speed.

The Conference ended and I caught the train for Vancouver. My journey was to be broken at Edmonton for a week's workshop and then a three-day weekend at Kamloops Junction. The trans-Canada train seemed more majestic than those of Australia. At first the scenery was rocks, lakes and woods, very picturesque and paintable. The prairies seemed to stretch for ever. They seemed dull, dun-coloured and flat, with low horizons and little to break the monotony, but after a while one's eye got acclimatised and noticed the movement of wind, the buffs, gold and tans with grey greens, cloud shadows from the immense expanse of sky as patterns on the grass changed rapidly. Once one was tuned in, the prairies had a beauty it would be a pleasure to record in paint.

I went to dinner with the Chairman of the Guild and her family in Edmonton and they told me of some old neighbours who had actually crossed the prairies by wagon in the pioneering days. My accommodation was in the university, which suited me very well. Workshops here were to deal with wall hangings and 3-D structures plus a design day. To my delight the Guild had members from Scandinavia and other countries with interesting textile histories. Skills were above average and some unusual adventurous projects took shape. With pupils who were competent my role was more that of a conductor of an orchestra than someone providing tuition. A restful change and a pleasant time, giving me ideas.

Embarking on the train again, the Rockies were the next visual treat. The train would pass through the most exciting mountains during the night so for this section of the journey I chose to have a seat by the window to watch. Rocks so close you could touch them, melting snow, streams with mini waterfalls sometimes splashing the train, gaps in the rock wall giving glimpses of every shape of white mountain peak, eerie blue shadows cast by the moon, more dark blue black lake fringed with fir trees. Almost too picturesque to bear. Sometimes I see these scenes in dreams still.

Kamloops and work was quite an anticlimax. I had a morning's sleep and then provided advisory tuition to a small group of friends. At the weekend, my half-sister Shirley arrived to drive me down to Vancouver. Part of the way along the Frazer Valley it was so hot that we could not get out of the air-conditioned car.

Vancouver had an assortment of workshops for the next three weeks. Shirley's house would be my home. She let rooms to girls from England who were finding their feet and new jobs before they found flats of their own. It was a cheerful company. I called the house Hansel and Gretel; it had a Bavarian look, gables with a pretty garden. It was situated in a tree-lined avenue of west Vancouver. Here the university befriended me. People kindly picked me up for the workshops. When Shirley's and my free time coincided she took me round all the sights and there were wonderful outings with the Guild to Indian settlements and museums. One day we went out strawberry picking to Richmond so that Shirley could stock up her freezer for the coming winter. Another sight I enjoyed was tree trunks floating in the water near the logging camps. It reminded me of the very early ship canal leading to Cardiff docks where goats and children skipped across on the floating logs and planks and tree trunks left there to season.

151

There was a week's workshop arranged by the Victoria Guild on Vancouver Island. I crossed in the Naimino ferry and was charmed by the Victorian appearance of the town. My host lived beside the coast and everything was made easy and pleasant. I did not realise at the time that this was the final workshop I would take overseas, so it was gratifying that it was successful. In fact, although in later years I had several small gatherings in my own house, the only large workshop was at Riverside, Lewes, for the Sussex Guild with Jenny Kilbride, when we had more than 20 pupils.

Shirley, plus her spaniel, came over to fetch me at the weekend. First we went to Butchards Gardens, a blossoming paradise planted to make the most of the landscape. It was staggering in the bright reds, pinks, mauves, purples, some blues all set off by white highlights. Father would have been entranced, not only in the display but also by the skilful planning. Two of Shirley's friends were babysitting a house and its pets, so we spent the night with them. Next day we crossed the island to Long Beach. Shirley had driven there a few years before, going down the old logging road, when her spaniel was still a puppy. Even though there was now a properly constructed road, Long Beach was still unspoilt – a motel and a cluster of huts and houses; miles and miles of wild, unspoilt beach; woods and green plants, edging rocks and shingle, leading to sandy patches with tree trunks and other flotsam lying around; small pools with seaweed, shells and crabs and other small fish. No one else was there but us.

The next day we travelled back to Vancouver and had a late dinner in the crowded Chinese quarter. This was a treat preparatory to packing up next day and catching the through train to Toronto. I just had time to visit a textile exhibition called 'Wall Hangings You Can Wear', or some such title, which influenced me years later. One exhibit was a marvellous semicircular cloak, spread out full on the wall. It was brilliant yellow in colour, an orange sun and abstract clouds, in very textured yarns. It made a fine wall hanging, but shown beside it was a large photograph of a model wearing it as a cloak. It must have impressed me, because years later in the 1980s I began to weave brocaded kimonos and caftans in the Moorman technique. My first was a kimono inspired by night and day. Someone saw it in an exhibition and gave me a commission for a larger version. There was another time interval and my weaving friend Enid Russ said an ex-pupil of hers had seen my kimono, hung on the wall as a decoration. I wear my own to this day!

The Rockies looked different in daylight on the journey back, equally impressive but in different colours. It was tiring doing the whole journey with not a break. I was spending a day or two with my god-daughter and her family and then treating myself to a visit to Niagara Falls. They were breathtaking and there was even a rainbow. But the next evening, as the Greyhound bus reached the top of a hill, there was an even more magical sight – New York skyscrapers touched with sunset colours, shown as they rose out of the mist silhouetted against the darkening western sky. More memorable and infinitely more beautiful than my first sight of the city from the sea.

My ex-Sherlock Holmes YW had not room for me so I sampled a more elegant version on Third Avenue. It was a shock to find that inside the plate glass front door one could see a Negro doorman sitting on a chair with a gun beside him. This door was kept locked from an early hour each evening. I had to ring for entry and even then convince him that I was a genuine resident. I rushed round New York, spending my last dollars and revisiting my favourite museums.

QEII was summer cruising by now so I had booked a berth, rather reluctantly, on the ill-fated liner SS *France*. This was to be her last but one voyage, although we did not know it, because her future was cut short by striking crewmen. However, it was to be the best voyage I ever made. She was a beautiful ship, most elegantly decorated and equipped. I shared a cabin most happily with a pleasant girl. The French, apparently, believed in pairing the young and old. It worked well because our timetable didn't clash. She got up about midday and came to bed with the dawn. I arose early for a swim and retired about midnight. We were expert at not waking each other. My table companions were very congenial; an American travelling alone to stay with her Italian husband's relatives near Verona, a Catholic priest, a genial businessman and a slightly unconventional lecturer. They were all well-read, interested in public affairs, art and literature and conversation was lively. We always took a long time as the head steward took an interest in our choice of menu and proffered suitable wines. It was quite rough so the dining room was fairly empty for the first two days. But as people recovered, we had to repel boarders. Many people cast an envious eye and at last one of those vivacious American widows, used to getting her own way, claimed the sixth seat at our table and blighted our meals. She talked incessantly. The priest appeared to listen politely and the rest of us concentrated on our food. It was the last night before Cherbourg, where three of the party were disembarking, so she had not gained much. Evening entertainment had been splendid, a French cabaret show, the latest film and a casino gambling evening.

I was quite sorry to leave the ship at Southampton. I dumped my luggage at Brighton and was off to the West Country for the family wedding. I felt I had earned a rest.

12

Retirement

After all the excitement of these workshop tours it was time to settle down to retirement. Not a happy future outlook for me. When I returned in summer 1974, it was the last moment of decision about selling my house and returning to the West Country. Now, 32 years later, it seems that it has been best to settle to stay in Brighton. At times I have been doubtful, but perhaps the excuse made for not taking a job in Australia – too far from London – was the underlying reason why I stayed put. I had fallen for my house at first sight, loved the garden and really enjoyed letting to students.

It hasn't proved to be the boring prospect it looked in the beginning. There was still my pad at Hornsey Lane, so I could go up at weekends to enjoy London life. The *Weavers Journal* needed someone to keep in contact with whoever was looking after its distribution, to see what exhibitions were on, and that became my job – as a runabout. In fact, when Win left, I became chairman of the editorial – again as stopgap. Here in Brighton I joined a gardening class at the Friends' Centre and managed to go back to the evening class at the art school to take up lithography, which I had started years ago at Hornsey and always enjoyed.

The gardening teacher from the Friends' Centre came to visit all her students' gardens. She was also interested in racing. Quite an interesting woman. When she came here to No. 1 Harrington Road, she told me two things about the garden a) my compost was excellent (she actually took some to show the rest of the class) and b) my glass greenhouse was unsafe and must be taken down. Later, I wished I had not asked her advice and taken it. That greenhouse could have been repaired. And when the north wing was sold to Longleys in about 1977 I had to purchase a shed to house my battery Webb mowing machine. It cost over £100. The Webb machine could have lived in the old greenhouse.

A tiny notice on the Friends' Centre noticeboard offered places at East Sussex County Council camp at Montrichard, France. One course was for art, the other French language appreciation. My application for art fell through – not enough support – but a place was made for me on the French course. The family had had caravans just after the war when the children were young, and I had joined them sleeping in a tent in both Devon and Cornwall, but that was some 20 years ago. I had enjoyed living in the open. Was I too old to begin to camp again?

My painter's sketchbook became a talisman and a comforter. Worries had been quite unnecessary, the holiday was bliss. I went camping at Montrichard every year with East Sussex until they gave up in the early 1980s. Greta Fenton was often the art tutor on these holidays. She loved Montrichard just as I did. When this camp closed she took over the organising of the holiday, and we had one last camp at Millet le Foret, close to Fontainebleau. Unfortunately Mrs Thatcher was attending an international conference that week at Fontainebleau so we never got a sketch of the chateau, but our surroundings were delightful. We had a day in Paris and a wonderful evening out when we joined their fête with the locals.

Greta joined up with another two adult art education teachers, Jane Weaver of the Friends' Centre and Maggie Corbin of Dupont, and together they organised sketching holidays in Arles, Avignon, Rouen, Amboise, Honfleur and so forth. I have not been fit to go away with them for the past two years, but in 1994 they went back to Montrichard and I joined them. This time it was living in a hotel in comfort.

People who don't draw miss out. A camera and snaps are not the same. The line in a quickie sketch gives instant recall of the place, the colour, even the smell and how one felt at that long ago moment. Sketchbooks are an evocative diary of one's life which you have for ever. Perhaps it is the mind, the eye and the hand all working together in absolute concentration that gives this vivid memory so long after. Paintings and drawings don't even have to be good for one to relive that past with pleasure. It all seems to be happening again. I can't say I didn't enjoy those hotel painting trips that we took later and of course I love holidays with my ex-art school friends, but nothing ever quite replaced camp life and the exhilarating absurdity of some of the disasters we survived.

One of the difficulties of retirement is the lack of a framework to every day each week and each season of the year. In anticipation this freedom looks most desirable. When you reach this stage it is bewildering. I can remember my little gran announcing on the day of Grandfather's funeral that she, in future, was going to live in her bedroom, stay in bed all day if she wanted to, and never come downstairs again. As a great concession she did make an appearance to see the flowers in the billiard room on the day of my mother's funeral, but for the rest of her life one visited her upstairs in her room.

Grandfather had been a large jovial man, a great playmate for his grandchildren making us all chuckle at the tales of his boyhood escapades with his two brothers. Little Gran was rather prim, delighting in her chapel and its minister; a splendid cook and one who enjoyed getting her own way. This new pattern of life was a belated rebellion at having to do so many things she disliked in modern life. My father's skills as a pianist were due to her indomitable will in dictating the hours he had to practise. In those comfortable days, at the beginning of this century, my grandparents' life had a daily framework, breakfast at 9, lunch at 1, afternoon tea at 4 and dinner at 7. Sunday was chapel, Monday – washday, Tuesday – shopping. On Wednesday Little Gran devoted the morning to cooking her special recipes for cakes and puddings, although she had two or three maids. One day would be set aside as an 'At Home' day when people came calling and left cards. Even the year had its pattern. All the family came home at Christmas. At Easter, the grandparents visited us, and when Father hired a house at the seaside for August, they stayed at a nearby hotel. It all seems so regimented, looking back from the free and easy life of today.

However, my working life was rather severely structured too. The studio regime was 9 – 5.30 weekdays, 9 – 12.30 Saturdays. Life with the navy was 24 hours allocated non-stop with about eight hours for eating and sleeping; the same pattern until seven days' leave happened about twice a year. In some ways teaching at an art school had a more flexible timetable, but when I first worked, giving part-time classes, it was 9.30 – 12, 2 – 4, teatime class 4.30 – 6.30, and evening class 7.30 – 9.30, four days a week. There was a spare three days to do one's own design work but one was pretty exhausted with the travel. Later, when I joined the full-time staff, life was easier and classes finished early.

No 1. Harrington Road.

It is no wonder that I needed some sort of framework to replace this timetable. My house, at No. 1 Harrington Road, Brighton, had always been too big for me to live in alone. It was in three units when I bought it: a self-contained garden flat, reasonably light, then the upper ground floor, consisting of the former drawing room with full-length sash windows opening onto the hooded balcony with steps to the garden. It is this aspect that reminds me of my grandparents' period house at 12 Maids Causeway, Cambridge, built circa 1789. This main room is now divided into a 15-foot-square sitting room and a kitchen/studio where I also have my loom. This division was made before I came to live here and spoils the proportion as the ceiling is pretty high. No. 5 Harrington Road, which was built at the same time as No. 1, still has the original layout of the ground floor and I have often longed to take the partition down and restore the room to its former glory. There were two marble fireplaces, one on the north wall and the other on the west wall, which is still in use today. It would, however, be an enormous room to heat and one person would feel lost and lonely.

I bought the house from a lady who had been born there. She described how there was a circular love seat upholstered in pink velvet standing in the middle of the room, with pink brocade long curtains to match at the windows. The entry hall has an openwork white wooden perforated archway, where the stairs begin, and I imagine that there were once crimson velvet curtains draped behind this, so draughts could be shut out from the upper floor. The room on the other side of the hall, now my bedroom, has also been altered, part made into a bathroom. In the old days there were two rooms, a study behind, with doors opening into the dining room which had a Regency bay window. In No. 5, these two rooms are in their original form. There is a north wing not belonging to me, built on towards the end of the nineteenth century, so the story goes, by a gentleman with five daughters to marry off. It consisted of one large ground floor room entered by a door from the original study, with three small bedrooms upstairs. This family only lived here about 10 years. They used the room for dances, musical evenings and amateur dramatics. When they had successfully disposed of the daughters, it was sold off to my landlady's grandparents and that family lived here until I came on the scene.

I lived in the ground floor flat for 18 months until the house was up for sale. I didn't like the look of the people who came to buy it, so cashed in my life assurance policies and bought the house in 1961. This gave me a sense of security and, of course, has proved an excellent investment. Old properties are expensive in upkeep. The year before the great storm, a main roof beam perished. There had to be a complete new roof, both timber and slates costing many thousands. It was a pity the storm didn't happen first. A year or two later, the hotel next door was doing interior alterations and knocked down a wall that had its counterpart in my house. That brought down the plaster ceiling in my bedroom. The bill for that was another £3,000 to replace the ceiling and redecorate. Compensation was only about £300.

Being one of a large family, I had never lived alone in a house, anywhere. First there was college, then YWCA, Bedford House in Baker Street, London, then shared flats followed by my time in WRNS quarters. When demobilised, I found bedsitting rooms in large Victorian houses with gardens to match. In all these homes there was a club-like atmosphere, so it was no hardship when I bought No. 1 to let the upstairs rooms, with their own kitchen and bathroom, to three young teachers when my landlady finally departed to her new cottage. After a few years teachers' salaries rose considerably so I turned to student letting. This kept me in touch with my teaching career and has been both a pleasure and an education to have all this young life bounding up and down stairs. When it gets a trifle overexuberant, there is always the long summer vacation in prospect to bring tranquillity for two or three months. Some students stay for just one year, some for two or three years. Occasionally the garden flat has students, but there have been some very happy long-term tenants there.

Before the house was mine, an elderly widow had been the tenant of the garden flat. She hadn't moved in very long before the house was put up for sale, and as neither her nor my agreement lease were very watertight, that must have been one of the reasons that influenced me to buy the house. Mrs Tilbury was a tremendous help in getting ready for the young tenants upstairs. My landlady, Nora Wynn, had had three cats and it was partly because they all got diseased and had to be put down that she sold the house. The whole place upstairs smelled of cat and for nearly a summer Mrs Tilbury and I used to scrub the floor, now bare planks, daily with disinfectant to really rid the place of the smell of them. She also came up and tidied my house for me while I was at work and this happy arrangement only ended with the first wedding of my tenants. She married a delightful man who had a jewellery and clock mending business up in the Midlands – Bedford. When they eventually sold the business in retirement they came back to Brighton and lived in a flat nearby. They would have come back to the garden flat, had it been one room bigger. Harry used to mend my clocks and his wife still kept an eye on what was happening here, laughing about all the tales of my students. A year or two after Harry died she came back to live in old age in Preston Park Nursing Home, opposite, which had been her cousin's house. She was pleased because she had the front bedroom there, which looked across the road and down my drive at the house and garden where she had been so happy.

The props to the framework needed to replace my timetable life were being found quite easily. When I first lived at No. 1, the adjoining house was Methuen Manor Nursing Home. The north wing was occupied by my landlady's elder sister, Constance Winchester. The owner of the nursing home would never believe that the south wing was mine, so I was glad when she gave up although it was quite eerie when it was unoccupied.

Down-and-outs and winos used to get food from the convent next door, breaking into the nursing home to try and live there. In my bath at night, where a shared chimney had always leaked sounds of the night sister telephoning the doctors, I would listen to voices of the intruders, then ring the police to chase them out. So it was very good when Mr and Mrs Barnes leased the property, did some renovations and turned it into the Touring Hotel. They were good neighbours. Jack would ring up and say, 'Painter Barnes asks Gardener Barker if he can come round with black sticky paint to patch their joint roof.' There was a way onto both our roofs via my attic window. We also shared part-time services of Mr Crawley, the expert local gardener. Some years later as I recounted earlier, the hotel was sold, Jack died suddenly abroad and Nan stayed on in my garden flat. Her two cats brought from the hotel, Top Cat and Twiggy, had eventually to be put down. They died of some mysterious, fast growing cancer, described by the vet as the same type that caused some musicians' deaths. It was the signal for Nan to buy her own flat in the next road, but sadly, she too died within a year of leaving here.

My family had suffered a tragedy too. My brother-in-law Ben was killed in a car crash, and what made this particularly distressing to us all was that my elder brother Norman had died in a similar accident almost to the day 20 years before. Ben and my younger brother Aubrey had been inseparable friends from kindergarten days so he was much closer to all the family than most brothers-in-law would be.

About this time my own legs gave trouble. I had five attacks of phlebitis, each one getting worse and climbing higher up the leg. So the specialist decided to strip the damaged veins. It was not much fun trying to walk with rigid plaster encasing both legs from top to bottom, almost like having two wooden legs. Luckily the op was a great success. A friend came down from London to look after me and I was soon weaving again.

My house was now home to five students, some staying just one year, some for the whole three years of their training. There was a happy spell with two art students in the garden flat, Anna and Phil. Anna had her twenty-first birthday in June and Phil borrowed white garden chairs from the hotel and put fairy lights up in the old apple tree. There was a party with music and all the trimmings for their friends. It was a magical evening and may have lasted until dawn, but I discreetly retired to the top attic, having enjoyed the transformation of my garden to wonderland. After a spell in London of a few years they married, came back to Brighton, bought a house and I still see them with their two small daughters.

Possibly the most successful tenancy of the garden flat for me was when a mature student taking his MA in computer sciences at Brighton Polytechnic asked if he could stay on after the degree course finished. I had always been reluctant to agree to students staying on because of complications with the Rent Act in case I needed to sell the house. My solicitors have always been instructed that whatever the date of my death, I did not want the house to be sold until the end of the summer term. This seemed only fair when one took student tenants. However, in this case, Ian had been a useful lodger, redecorating the flat and helping in the garden. So when he got a job at Lewes, I agreed that he could stay on indefinitely. That was over seven years ago and my decision has turned out to be a wise one. He has always been a great practical help and also taken a comforting interest in the doings of students in the upstairs flat. I can vent my indignation at their occasional misdeeds to him, and the conversation always ends in laughter, just as it had in the days of Mrs Tilbury and Nan.

When my right hip had to be replaced, he supervised my learning to walk again. Unfortunately, four months later I had a stroke and again Ian helped me regain confidence to recover. My sisters are most grateful to him for his care of me. For myself, it made it possible to stay on in my house over a difficult 18 months and I am everlastingly grateful to Ian for this. In 1994, he left to work in Australia and the flat was let to students again for one last year.

After that stroke, which damaged my eye, mouth and throat – I also had more difficulty in walking – my artist friends rallied round to help me get back to normal. Greta took me on the sketching outings and I joined the University of the Third Age sketch club. Beryl took over my cleaning and gardening, and much more important than that, built up my shaken confidence so I could go out alone again. It has been wonderful to have such friends. The Health Club next door has been most kind in encouraging me. Everyone next door looks me up and down critically, and says, 'That eye is better today,' or 'Are you doing your facial exercises?' They have been so kind that I quickly got used to being disfigured and now get praised for looking almost normal again.

Another prop in finding a substitute to the old timetable life has been researching family history. I got hooked on this quite by chance. My cousin and his wife, together with Sylvia, the daughter of the adopted daughter of our great-uncle Willie, a marvellous old boy whom we all knew (he did not die until the 1930s), were going to Cambridge to the university library to look at Bishops' transcripts for Waterbeach. This village we knew well from our childhood days, when it was always referred to as the family village. I went with them, just for the holiday. The first day it thrilled me, examining early documents in the university library, noting down both Barker and Norman names, in case they were ancestors. I searched a card index there and found a will for Peter Barker of Waterbeach, dated 1400. I knew a Peter Barker, son of my father's cousin, who was an agricultural officer. Could we be descended from the first Peter, also a farmer? Sadly, when later I got a copy of this will, Peter only named daughters. Still, he might have had brothers who survived.

We had an appointment to meet the Vicar at Waterbeach that afternoon. Over lunch in the library canteen, I remembered grandfather taking me, aged about seven, to see his grand-mother's grave because I was named for her. This was at Great Chesterford so Kenneth said we could go there to find out why she was buried there and not in Waterbeach. When we got to that village someone opened the iron gate leading to the church. It squeaked and that brought back instant memory. 'It's up the path on the little mound,' I said, triumphant. And so it was.

Waterbeach was also a success. We were waiting for the Vicar in that churchyard beside two gravestones leaning against the wall. One was for that Mary Barker's husband and the other for his father. In the church, the Vicar produced not only the parish registers but one vellum book dating back to Henry VII. I then had a fascinating new hobby, taking me to record offices in Cambridge and Lewes, also the Public Records Office in London and the Society of Genealogists. I have thoroughly enjoyed the never-ending research and still belong to the Sussex Family History Society.

Backing up all these other interests has been the East Sussex Guild of Weavers, Spinners and Dyers. I always think of it as my Guild because it grew out of the Brighton Branch of Sussex Guild, which covered Worthing and Hastings as well. Several members came to my evening classes at Brighton College of Art from 1950. I must have joined soon after and am probably the longest surviving member, bar Dorothy Ablett. I think I succeed-ed Valentine Kilbride as Chairman and Dorothy was then Secretary. I gave up when embarking on those years of overseas travel but rejoined soon after the Guild became so much larger it left the Friends' Centre in Brighton for Riverside at Lewes. At one stage I was Treasurer for a year until David and Sonia (Barnett) took over and then Vice Chairman for a while until the Guild did me the honour of electing me President.

In summer 1992 they gave me a tape recorder to write my life story. This has taken a long time as progress was hindered by my hip operation and the following stroke. I can never thank the Guild enough for their support and comfort, which have helped my recovery. Long may they continue their kindly help to any members who are in sickness or loss.

Old age seems to divide people into those who do too little and those who do too much. My observation has suggested that those who overdo it have a pleasanter life and usually last longer. However, having always had a timetable/clocking-in type of life – school, work, navy, teaching – I found it easier to have a regular target to rebel against. In my really old age, the hotel next door put up a health centre with a swimming pool in the back garden. The waste water comes down my drains, which are the same ones as when the house was built in the 1840s. At the time I was furiously indignant at this trespass, but my Monday to Friday 9 o'clock swim gives a tidy start to a well-filled day and prevents me ever following my little gran's example until my legs give out.

When my garden flat lodger left for Australia in September 1994 the garden flat had students again. I began the session with five, a full house. Upstairs there were two English boys and a girl, Regina, from Botswana. They were doing second year computer sciences. The boys had befriended Regina and looked after her well. Unfortunately Dan failed his Christmas tests and as he had also failed his first year test in summer 1994, he was told to leave his course. In February James did not get on so well with Regina so she found another lodging at Easter.

While my three remaining tenants were revising for their summer term tests, I fainted and dislocated my new hip. I pressed my Care Link and they sent an ambulance to take me to hospital for three weeks. My tenants left during this time but they behaved admirably – with motherly and grandmotherly help, the flats were spring-cleaned properly. They looked cleaner than ever before. Sadly, my name was removed from the university lodgings list by the accommodation officer because two students had left.

It seemed the right moment to go so my house is up for sale and I am having fun flat-hunting again. Perhaps I shall know in an instant like I did with No. 1 Harrington Road when it is the right home for me.

During the winter of 1994 someone interviewed me for the National Life Story collection of the British Library. I ended the interview with the spontaneous statement, 'What fun it's been to be me!'

13

MBE

Have you ever felt on waking up 'What fun it is to be me' or, 'Can't possibly cope with what is to happen today?' On 22 July 1992 both sensations hit me simultaneously when my niece Carol woke me up. This was the day I was to go to Buckingham Palace to be decorated with the MBE by the Queen.

My half-sister when small had a telling expression when she was made to do something she didn't like to do: 'It's aggustingly unfair' – a cry of protest against an unkind fate. Today I understood exactly what she meant. Life is like that. Why should this be happening to me when awaiting a hip operation? Fancy managing a lonely walk on a slippery floor, a bob curtsey step backwards and another curtsey. Reason told me, it's all your own fault. You need not have said 'yes' to the Prime Minister's offer. You could have accepted the specialist's suggestion to operate on your hip in May. He had laughed at my refusal and said it was the first time he had been given that excuse. He suggested one or two sticks. No way! Worse still, I was not going to wear my best new printed Jaeger skirt because it had seemed impossible to find the right top for it. My choice was an old summer three-piece which had done duty on many an evening abroad, only because I had cherished a model hat bequeathed to me by a friend's mother. This suited me and was the right colour. An oldish pair of summer sandals were my only safe footwear; not a confidence uplift from one's outfit. It did not much help when Carol appeared looking super in the latest fashion, an elegant green-bordered navy outfit with picture hat.

We had a dicey journey traffic-wise, cross-country from Richmond to Clapham to pick up my nephew Christopher, complete in morning dress, top hat and all. I felt a little pinky beige mouse accompanied by such splendour. We did arrive at the Palace at the correct time, after all. I had disclosed my disability to St James's Palace and they had given me a special sticker so we could go straight up in the lift from the Duke of York's entrance. Christopher flummoxed the young footman – no history scholar – by asking which Duke of York. We were led along a corridor the length of the inner quadrangle. One side was lined with priceless antiques and Royal Family portraits, the other by windows. No time to gaze. This manoeuvre was to avoid me walking up the long staircase from the main entrance. That meant we missed an impressive sight, but I had seen this at the end of the Second World War when my brother Norman came with me to see Stepmama get a Red Cross decoration from the then Queen Elizabeth, now the Queen Mother. She had kept up a lively conversation with her entourage while dealing out medals and shaking hands, so everyone felt at home.

My guests left me for their seats in tiers surrounding the ballroom, where they would be entertained with light music played by a Guards band situated in the balcony. I was directed to the Picture Gallery and was nervously crossing the shiny parquet floor of the ante-room when there was an awful warning. Just in front of me a large lady in bright green suddenly fell with a mighty wallop. Two tall Chinese vases worth at least a million stood on plinths either side of the archway ahead. They swayed alarmingly. A query flashed through my mind. Does one dash forward to try to save a vase from disaster or should one try to hoist the green job to her feet? Luckily the vases righted themselves, elegant aides obviously used to such catastrophes rushed to help the lady up and pop her white boater hat back at just the wrong angle, while my aching hip rooted me to the spot. After this it was slow march for me, each step a careful effort.

We were divided like sheep into pens separated by crimson ropes held up on brass posts. 'Women's Lib' would have been horrified. The green lady seemed the only female in the CBE pen.

There were only seven of us among upwards of forty men in our group; not a high proportion. The Knights-to-be had been siphoned off into a side room. Their drill must have been more terrifying than ours. Christopher afterwards described with glee how the Queen dealt with them. They knelt before her and she held out her right hand for the sword from her equerry. She swung it expertly round their heads touching each shoulder in turn, then without looking tossed it back to the waiting officer. Practice makes perfect. Christopher longed to know if the sword had ever slipped a bit and nicked an ear or two.

It was a long and tantalising wait between 10 and 11 a.m. Tantalising because one was surrounded by priceless historic paintings without the freedom to wander about and study them closely. Luckily one side of our pen was lined with gilt sofas upholstered in grey and white satin stripes. I sat down on one with the best view and was quickly joined by another 'oldie'. Her outfit was neat and new, a navy top with white pleated skirt edged with a two-inch band of navy, topped with a small blue hat. Her homely comments on our fellows were a joy. Men had the advantage; the young officers looked supreme, well groomed in their best uniforms, other ranks gleaming with 'spit and polish'. There were a couple of actors, perfectly turned out, one black, one white, with contemporary haircuts. My Wren experience naturally awarded the prize to two naval medical officers and it was somehow reassuring that when our group was mustered and led out of the pen, it was headed by these two.

After all this masculine splendour, we ladies made a doubtful showing. Men had had a hook hung onto their left breast pocket on which the Queen would place their medal. Quite easy. We were more of a problem. A charming lady-in-waiting did her best to pin our hooks in a like position but our flimsy finery made this insecure and she usually had to fasten it through to a bra strap. No one seemed to have thought about the magnificent scarlet, gold and white surroundings when choosing an outfit. One woman had a red top – vermilion – which clashed with scarlet and crimson, her large picture hat was trimmed with white organdie flowers, and as a finish, another floral spray, almost

169

bridal, decorated her small red handbag, which she refused to relinquish when we were asked to hand in our bags. The youngest lady had a pretty peach blazer with a full printed floral skirt, sadly with not enough petticoat. I envied her her delightful high-heeled sandals, but hoped she would be able to balance when she curtseyed. A recently retired Civil Servant was discreetly clad in navy with a small white pattern on the skirt.

Ten to eleven o'clock was a long desert of time. I longed for a cup of coffee. Nerves began to show, chatter died out, people fidgeted and my perky friend announced she smelt fear. Suddenly a court official of high rank appeared in the space between our two pens and announced he was going to demonstrate exactly what we had to do. The drill was that an official would send you forward to a marker. You listened for your name to be called, advanced to a mat, did a left turn, bowed (or in our case, curtseyed) to the Queen, then walked a step or two forward to the dais. She would bend forward to hang your medal on your hook and speak to you. You answered saying, 'Your Majesty' the first time and 'Ma'am' afterwards. In dismissal she then shook your hand. You walked backwards to the end of the rug, curtseyed, turned right and walked out of the ballroom, had your medal and hook removed and your handbag returned with the medal in a case. You were then sent back to the rear of the ballroom to sit and watch those who came after. He demonstrated this twice, laughed as he told us he could not show us how to curtsey, and disappeared.

Suddenly the CBE pen emptied. Then it was our turn to be mustered and led away, the ladies all in a group in alphabetical order. It was too fast for me. I tried to dawdle and get a closer look at the paintings, but to no avail. Crossing the back of the ballroom rapidly, we all looked anxiously for our relatives seated in tiers down each side. Carol and Christopher saw me and waved. There was then another wait, standing this time, but a kindly official stood by answering our questions. He explained that they had these investitures eight or more times each year and the routine worked like clockwork – he and his fellows wanted us to enjoy our investiture. At last our guardian said, 'It's your turn now,' and in no time being number three in alphabetical order, I was standing in the doorway watching the victim ahead. 'You'll be all right,' said the official as he sent me on my way. It was unnerving waiting for one's name to be read out – but easy when the moment came. My curtsey was fine – not a twinge from my hip – and there was the Queen bending down with the medal and giving the hook a little tug to see it was safely fixed. She was smiling and said, 'Still weaving?' just like any of my friends. Then she asked what sort of things I wove. A hidden video camera was taking photographs and one can see by those how friendly she was and how easy it was to talk to her. Also it was pleasant to see that her dress was a soft blue with small spots edged pink that blended well with my old summer suit. A firm hand grip and I somehow managed to step backwards and curtsey again. She had joined HMS *President III's* Sea Rangers when we were stationed at Windsor during World War II so I had met her before.

After this it was anticlimax. We were sent to the back of the ballroom to sit on hard chairs. There were so many seated ahead we could not see what was happening, and under cover of the music we had a chat with our neighbours. Then suddenly we had to leap to our feet for *God Save the Queen*, and she departed flanked by two Beefeaters in their traditional uniform carrying halberds.

There was quite a stampede as people collected their relatives and made a dash downstairs to get a good place in the official photograph queue. We found our footman and he led us back to the lift. Collecting our belongings, which had been sitting unsearched on a priceless cabinet in lacquer and ormolu, Carol produced her camera. A friendly policeman said he was not allowed to take our photograph but found an air force chauffeur to do this. Walking through the archway across the courtyard there was a crowd of observers waiting outside the railings. Christopher's top hat quickly found us a taxi and we were off to Carol and Richard's City Circle restaurant for lunch. There champagne awaited us, my great-niece Sally rushed up to greet me and many of their regular customers joined in the congratulations. It was a lovely family occasion to mark the day and we had a celebration lunch. It hardly seemed believable that all this had

171

happened to me. I was in a dreamlike state travelling to Sydenham to spend the night with a friend. Then reality struck and my wretched hip played up, but all in all it had been a day out of time to remember.

14

Weaving Workshops Overseas

My workshop programme during my overseas visits described earlier was to show how exciting quality fabrics could be woven on four-shaft looms. My students had been very successful in winning Royal Society of Arts bursaries with fabric designs for both women's and men's wear as well as furnishings. In my early teaching career yarns had been very limited – I do remember as a student at Hornsey College of Art solemnly degreasing sea boot stocking wool and painstakingly dyeing small skeins of rich colour in order to weave a small tapestry. Most yarns were on coupons because of war conditions. As soon as possible, I began stocking the weaving department cupboards with remainders from manufacturers – some old friends from the past. In this way an exciting collection was built up. There might not be enough for mass production but there was certainly enough for samples. The mini sum of money afforded by college authority was spent on buying the basic yarns. My remainders were mostly given free. The prizewinning students helped too. The Royal Society of Arts arranged a foreign tour for them, visiting museums and textile manufacturers. As they were prudent administrators there was always some money left unspent, so this was used to send the students on a visit to manufacturers here, who would give the students any leftover yarns and often send me a sack or two for the next year's intake. In 21 years our cupboards at Brighton were full to overflowing, so I secreted a few extra special spools of yarn among my luggage.

My students had from the beginning been taught to design for specific purposes. One week it would be to plan a coat fabric for Jaeger. The following might be for a range of tweed in four different colourways for mass production. It always had seemed to me important to target the manufacturer, not to design in a vacuum.

I had no idea of what the situation would be in Australia and New Zealand. Some of my friends had had very successful workshop tours in America but they had always demonstrated their own special technique. I was going to 'play the field', to take on a dozen cloth constructions expecting some original results, a tall order by any standard. My first workshop in Wellington taught me some basic lessons. First, that the number of students and their varied speed were a help – not a worry. One just picked on the one who finished her orthodox sample first, sat down at her loom, gathering everyone around, and demonstrated ways of varying the weave. By the time I had messed up some five or six inches of her precious warp, everyone was dashing back to her own loom to finish the correct sample and then have a go at trying something different. Luckily their varied speeds spaced them out so I could give individual attention where needed. In workshops where there were spare looms set up, life was not so hectic.

A selection of the drafts and warp particulars that were sent in advance to one Guild is shown here. This was done so that looms could be prepared ready for my arrival to avoid wasting time. These particulars were copied from the cards I made to hang on each loom. It was a stipulation that no beginners were to be enrolled; there was to be a maximum of 12 students and 14 or 15 looms. If drafts were to be duplicated, there were to be two very different yarns chosen.

My last term at Brighton Polytechnic had been so hectic that these drafts were not completed by the sailing date, so until Cape Town, where they must be posted to arrive in time, my shipboard routine was breakfast, keep-fit class, swim, then dash to the peace and quiet of the library and get down to work. Fortunately, the liner only put in at Rotterdam, Freetown then South Africa en route, so shore visits did not interrupt my task too often.

174

The problems of running a workshop with unfamiliar yarns and doubtful setts (number of ends per inch) on looms of varied construction were enough to daunt a more optimistic character than myself. Often I would be arriving by plane the night before, staying with strangers, perhaps only having a few minutes to look at the looms while the students were gathering. Looking back, to my surprise I cannot remember any insurmountable difficulties. One or two looms would be set too openly and need the reed to be rethreaded. Sometimes when thicker fancy yarns or homespun were used as features in a warp, it was necessary to change the reed to a coarser one, say replacing a 14 dent reed with a 6 or 8 one. This would involve the thick thread having a dent to itself while the finer one would be entered into two per dent. Once or twice the way a loom was built made it easier to weave the stock pattern upside down but that was no hardship.

The workshop was to run for three consecutive days. The first one was in Wellington, New Zealand. It got off to a slow start as some students were reluctant to weave the stock pattern for 6 inches before experimenting, and wilfully went their own way. At first, I allowed this with the ringleaders, but after a docile member had finished her warp with 6 inches of the orthodox pattern and two experimental samples of reasonable size to be mounted, there was little further rebellion. There were not so many Weaver's Guilds in those days and word got around on the grapevine that many good ideas were spoiled by not weaving at least 4 inches.

Changing looms was also a problem because of variations in speed of the weavers. This was where the extra looms proved useful. We hung up a list of people who wanted to weave a sample on a popular draft, and where needed a spare loom was set up overnight. As everyone had a copy of the drafts, they could always try them out at home.

On the third day at lunchtime, all the warps were cut off and where necessary given a wet finish. In the afternoon, they were cut up and divided among their various owners. I found it paid dividends to get as many mounted with full particulars as possible and we often had a show for the local Guild. The enthusiasm everywhere was very rewarding.

First are shown three suggestions for threading up rigid heddle looms; these only give two lifts, up alternate threads, then down. This is made by a hole in the bar of the reed followed by a slit. These are usually made to give a sett of 12 threads per inch. For rug weaving, a sett of 6 ends per inch would work for samples. This sett was achieved by filling a hole, then a slit, then missing a hole and a slit. Rugs are usually weft faced, the weft being beaten down to cover the warp ends completely. The sample could be woven in colour stripes or the effect of one light pick of rug wool followed by a dark single, then a batch of two light, two dark and various combinations. It was useful to use for teaching Soumak, Rya and all assorted knots, pick-ups and inlay, or a simple tapestry.

The next loom was warped up in a plain 2 ply cotton alternating with a gimp thread, all in white. There was a note given on the instructions that the fancy yarn was not to be too rough to pass through the heddle reed. Surprisingly this last warp turned out a great success when used for finger gauzes and grouped weaves such as Brooks Bouquet.

A further development can be made on a rigid heddle loom by using it for a space warp, using different combinations of the following:

a) Normal threading

b) Doubling up the number of threads in a hole and slit

c) Leaving a space empty

d) Using several threads through a slit to make a cord

When a space warp is designed for a four-shaft loom, two rules are needed:

- the open sett must be held between A, B or D to prevent slipping

- D must be used sparingly as a feature or else it causes difficulty in shedding.

Also it was found that when a normal sett for A was 20 ends per inch, the loom would not shed properly when too much space was given to B; so that had to be reduced to 30 ends per inch.

As a general rule, half to one inch worked best as spaces left unfilled in the reed. Plain weave is usually best for such drafts.

APPENDIX

Weaving Workshop Drawdowns

RIGID HEDDLE THREADINGS

I. for Rug Samples

WARP   length 3yds of string 2 ply flax
            width   6"

            Sett 6 ends per inch   fill hole   fill space
                                        leave hole   leave space

            Total number of ends: 6 × 6 = 36

II. Basket Check

WARP   length 3 yds of black and white gimp
            width 6"

            Sett 12 ends per 1"

            Total number of ends: 6 × 12 = 72

Colour order of warp: 1 black 1 white repeat 6 times
                             1 white 1 black repeat 6 times

III.   Space Warp for finger weaves

WARP   length 3 yds
                    width 6″

                    Sett 12 ends per 1″

                    Total number of ends: $13 \times 6 = 78$

Reed – fill $\frac{1}{2}$″ 1 fancy   1 cotton;   leave $\frac{1}{2}$″ empty
        N.B. fancy must not be too rough to pass through
            reed

SPACE WARP

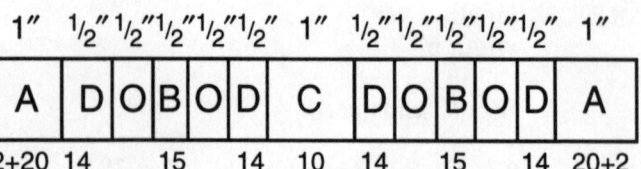

A	D	O	B	O	D	C	D	O	B	O	D	A

2+20 14 15 14 10 14 15 14 20+2

DRAFT FOR
A. B. C

DRAFT FOR
D

Warp   length 4yds of cotton or linen 2/12s or finer
width 8″

Sett in 10 dent reed   A. normal 20 ends per 1″
B. close 30 ends per 1″
C. open 10 ends per 1″
D. cords 28 ends per 1″
O. space

Total number of ends (see diagram)   136
Selvedge double outside two   4
                                     140

180

WEAVE plain

There are 14 different lifts possible with a four-shaft loom, and throughout history, tradition from many countries has shown what varied use can be made of them. Conservatively, these lifts are used for:

plain weave	1 and 3
	2 and 4
2/2 twill	1 and 2
	2 and 3
	3 and 4
	4 and 1
3/1 twill	123-
	-234
	1-34
	12-4
1/3 twill	1
	2
	3
	4

The next two warps for four-shaft looms in my programme were herringbones showing the change in thickness and the second change in length of slant. The characteristic feature of herringbone weave is the 'cut' where it changes direction. This differentiates it from point draft which has a float of three that is a weakness.

VARIATIONS IN HERRINGBONE (Appendix pp 2 and 3)

The first point to notice in weaving herringbone is the definite cut where the slopes change direction. This is the reason why herringbone is so useful a weave. Woven in two and two twill order, it gives a smooth strong fabric which, if fine yarns are used, drapes well. Traditionally used for men's suitings, it can give plenty of variation if woven in unorthodox lifts.

181

With the change of direction and length of slope draft, we tried introducing two threads of a different colour where the slopes changed direction. Plain weave or tabby cannot be woven on this draft but alternating lifts one and three with two and four produces an interesting effect.

The thickness of the two yarns chosen for the second draft works best at two to one. This often needs the thick thread to be entered singly through the reed while the finer one is entered in twos. I had intended these two drafts, both interesting in set weave, to be ones quickly woven for 6 inches in the changeover situation but some pupils found them worthy of experiment.

Although plain weave has more intersections than two and two twill, making it the strongest cloth structure, the latter is useful as it tailors well, but also in fine yarns it drapes wonderfully.

HERRINGBONE – *change in thickness*

WARP   length   4yds
               width   6″

Sett 20 ends per 1″ – 2 through each dent
10 dent reed

Total number of ends 20 x 6	120
Selvedge double outside two	4
	124

Warp yarns – tweed, woollens or homespun

This tweed weave can be classed with twills and hopsacks as the next in strength of cloth structure to plain weave.
Woven in 2/2 twill order the floats are never more than two, unlike point draft which has a three float. There is a definite cut where slope changes direction.

Variations   A.   Change in length of slope
                   B.   Change in thickness
                   C.   Change colour with each change of slope

Weave Suggestions   (i)   2/2 twill
                       (ii)   3/1 twill
                       (iii) Diamond – 12 picks 2/2 twill, cut and
                                       12 picks reverse
                       (iv) Thin and thick picks 1.2.3.4. as draft
                       (v)   Rethread reed – open and crowded
                       (vi) 'Hiccup' 20 picks 2/2 twill cut
                                         6 picks reverse twill

HERRINGBONE – change in length

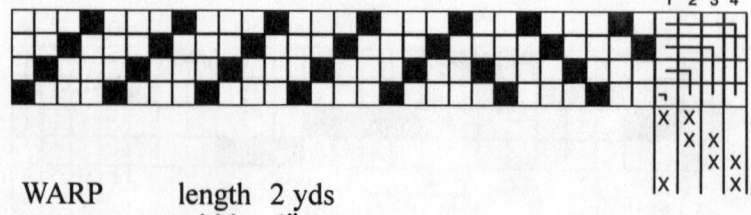

WARP   length   2 yds
              width   6″

              Sett 28 ends per 1″ – 2 through each dent
              14 dent reed

              Total number of ends 28 x 6   168
              Selvedge double outside two   4
                                                  172

Warp yarns – tweed, woollens or homespun

WAFFLE WEAVE

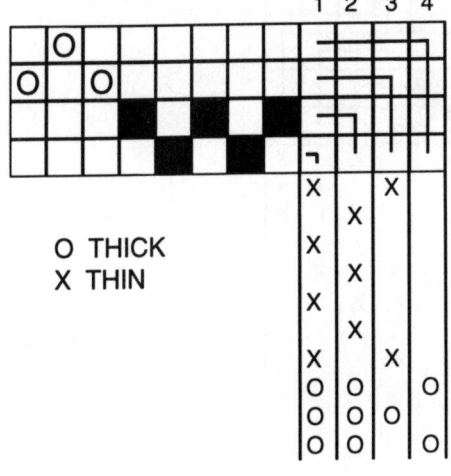

For thick yarn use homespun or boucle

for thin yarn use wool

O THICK
X THIN

WARP   length   4 yds
        width   6″

Sett 20 ends per inch – 2 through each dent
10 dent reed

Total number of ends: 20 x 6 = 120 + 5 to level   125
Selvedge double outside two   4
                                                   ───
                                                   129

Colour order 5 dark thin 3 thick light threads

This is a versatile draft – depends on use of thick and thin yarn.
One student did 32 variations in weaving this.

Suggest thick yarn is best at least four times the thickness of
ground yarn. An extra lurex thread on the first and last end and
lift of shaft 2 gives an attractive highlight.

185

CANVAS or MOCK LENO

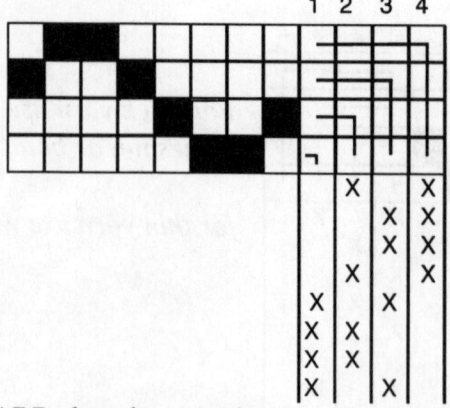

WARP   length   4 yds
            width   8″

          Sett 20 ends per 1″ in a 10 dent reed sleyed as follows
             first 4″ – 2 ends per dent
             second 4″ – 4 ends per dent – leave 1 dent empty

          Total number of ends: 20 x 8 = 160
YARN   cotton or linen
            wool if smooth

To get an open mesh effect, group 4 ends in one dent in reed, leave one empty. Suggest half sample is reeded thus and the other half 2 per dent taking care not to split the two ends that work together.

Shafts 1 and 3 opposing shafts 2 and 4 do not give true tabby or plain weave but interesting non tabby structures can be made.

Try fancy wefts.

SWEDISH POINT or Monks Belt

1   2   3   4

WARP   length   4 yds   O thick yarn
          width   6″

Sett 20 ends per 1″ – 2 through each dent 10 dent reed

Total number of ends:
20 x 6 = 120 + 10 to balance   130
Selvedge double outside two   4
                           134

YARN   2/6s cotton or linen or equivalent wool
          Colour order – 10 Black 10 White

A distorted weft effect can be woven on four shafts. Different colour in waved patches.

WEFT   1 pick thick red yarn
          7 picks black
          2 picks thick red yarn
          7 picks white
          1 pick thick red yarn

Beat cloth firmly after each thick plain weave pick. This should then bend round plain weave patch of black & white.

There are many other variations on this draft.

Try using a tabby binder of same thickness as warp with 4 gold pattern weft repeated on shafts 1 and 2 ten times. Then shafts 3 and 4 ten times.
The tabby binder must be used in correct sequence first 1 and 3, then 2 and 4.

187

DOUBLE CORDUROY

O Thick yarn for loops

for easier threading think of draft in groups of five ends

WARP	length	4 yds
	width	6"

Sett at 20 ends per 1"

Total number of ends: 20 x 6	=	126
Selvedge double outside two		4
		130

YARNS suggest tweed or knitting wool 2 ply for warp
fancy wool or homespun used fourfold as pile weft

Variation: 2/6s cotton or linen for warp at 10 ends per 1"
Weft: raffia – raw flax – natural fibres etc.

RUGS 6/10s lea linen warp
Sett 6 ends per inch low pile
" 4 " " " long shaggy pile

Ground weft 6 ply rug wool
Pile " 6 fold with 6 epi
" " 9 " " 4 epi

This technique adapts well for furnishing, either loops or cut, all over or in pile stripes. There are always selvedge difficulties with pile.
N.B. After each pile pick, pull up weft as difficult to cut if left flat.

188

Waffle

This is a versatile draft, with the weave given; it makes a cloth with surface interest, a dimpled effect. In extreme yarns, it becomes a distorted cloth.

Mock Leno

In true Leno or gauze weave, one warp thread in each group is brought up first one side of another warp thread by a doup shaft. This can be made on a four-shaft table loom with a certain amount of difficulty. This produces small holes in the fabric. Mock Leno with spaces left in the reed gets its name because it gives a similar first look with similar holes.

Swedish Lace

I included this weave expecting it to be used in traditional manner as it is an example of every other thread put onto the same shaft. The loom usually works best if this is the second shaft. To my surprise, using finger gauzes with a thicker thread, and only lifting section B for a square, interesting dress fabrics were produced. It would be possible, weaving most of a dress in plain weave, to make the top decorative with openwork squares at intervals. This was an example of designing on a four-shaft loom for a fabric which could be woven more easily on eight shafts and a treadle loom when going into yardage.

Monks Belt or Swedish Point

This is a well-known draft, simple but giving many variations of its characteristic pattern.

Double Corduroy

At the tea interval in Wellington on my first visit when I was giving a criticism to a Guild on its work, they had talked eagerly about Double Corduroy rugs, a technique that Peter Collingwood's book *The Technology of Rug Weaving* had explained very thoroughly. I said idly that I had not seen one yet.

There was a shocked silence, and a Yorkshire lass – expatriates always rally round me on these occasions – nudged me and said, 'You are standing on one'. I looked down at the thin wispy object I was standing on, mentally comparing it with the full rich rugs I was used to seeing at home, and said without thinking, with scorn, 'That is not Double Corduroy'. The members all crowded round defending its maker and assured me it was. Apparently, a well-known local teacher had travelled far and wide Down Under, teaching her version. I had to include this draft in workshops, and try to correct her error. At first no one believed me – their teacher had been very dogmatic – but fortunately my hostess for that weekend had a treadle loom set up ready to weave a Double Corduroy rug. I sat down and wove a true version, using 2 ply carpet wool six fold for the Corduroy sheds, pulling the float up between the tie down sections. When 9 inches had been woven, I laboriously cut the floats dead centre. After that there was no more argument. The word passed round. Curiously, this was one of the least popular drafts in my workshops.

Double Cloth

To me, this draft leads to advanced weaving. It is possible to weave on four shafts and get an understanding of the principle in construction, but to get full use eight shafts are needed. A great many hand weavers were using this technique to double the width of fabric woven on their loom. To me this is a mistake; one can always detect the turning point. I did meet one Australian weaver, ex-Austrian trained by an ex-Bauhaus teacher, who was weaving coverlets on a wide loom, opening up to get double width, but she used an ingenious warp plan - doubling up threads at intervals – and this did disguise the turning point fairly well.

Anyway, Double Cloth on four shafts was one of the most popular drafts in all my workshops.

COUNTERPOINT TWILL

■ Fine yarns
O Thick yarns

Sample

Warp Length 4 yards
    Width 6 inches
    Sett 20 ends per inch
    Reed 10 dent sleyed 2 ends per dent
    Selvedge Double outside two Rt hand side of warp
      and add 4 fine threads for Lt hand edge
    Yarn order 2 fine ends
              2 thick ends
    Yarns II cut wool for fine
        3 ply knitting or fancy for thick

A draft was constructed using thick yarn for a twill running from left to right filling in the spaces with a right-hand twill in finer yarn. As this was to be used for planning coatings, two thicker yarns were entered side by side. This worked very well, producing exciting Jaeger type reversible fabrics. It was an opportunity to use handspun yarns for the thicker thread.

Swedish Lace

This is an example of a weave with every other thread on shaft two. The threading sequence A gives plain weave using A lift, B will give openwork stripes vertically and C stripes horizontally. The draft is traditionally woven in linen for table mats. The threading sequence given in the diagram was a mini-version to suit the number of heddles on each shaft of the average table loom. Once weavers got the right beat of the batten to keep the cloth even, this draft wove well.

To my delight, the adventurous weavers found other ways of designing with a blend of horizontal and vertical stripes. One lady even used a finger weave gauze on every sixth pick. We decided this could be used as the yoke on a child's dress with the body woven in plain weave.

SWEDISH LACE BORDER

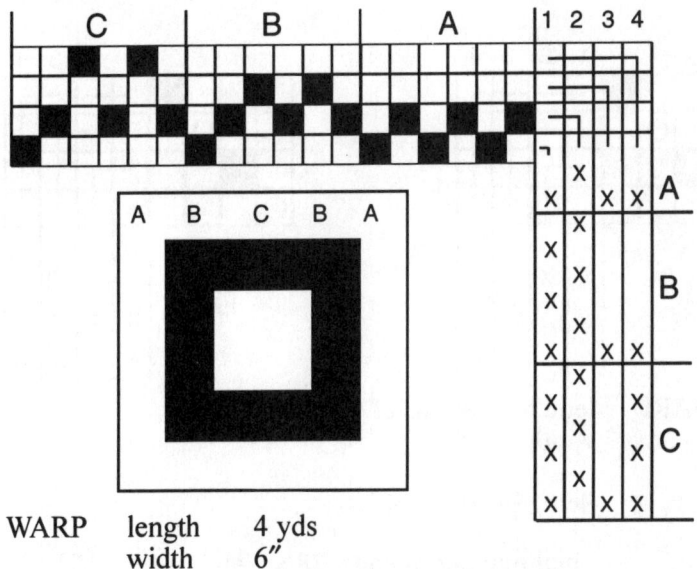

WARP   length   4 yds
               width   6″

Sett 24 ends per inch – 2 through each dent 12 dent reed

Total number of ends 24 x 6   144
Selvedge double outside two   4
                                               148

YARN   2/8s linen or 2/6s cotton

Threading Sequence			*Weave*	
A. 24 ends	(four repeats)		A. 24 picks	
B. 24	″	(four repeats)	B. 24	″
C. 48	″	(eight repeats)	C. 48	″
B. 24	″	(four repeats)	B. 24	″
A. 24	″	(four repeats)	A. 24	″

An interesting principle depending on every other end being on the second shaft. Although this is a traditional technique, there are many interesting variations

193

DOUBLE CLOTH

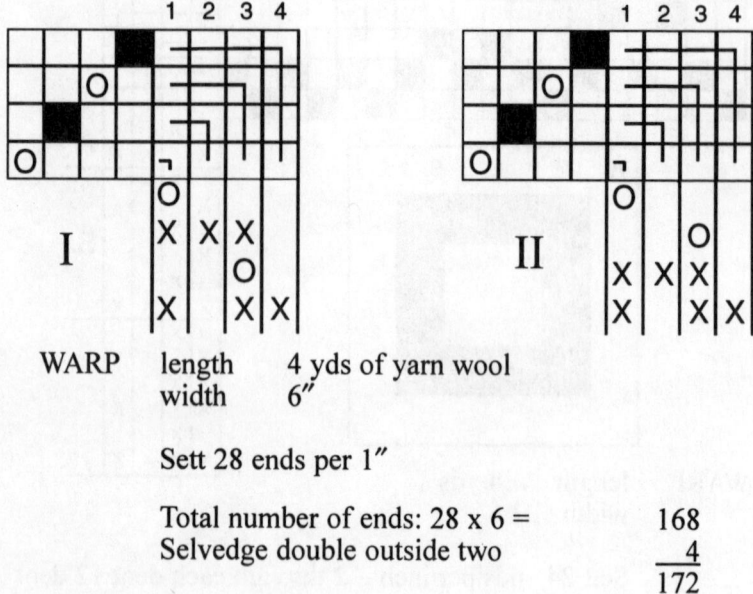

WARP   length   4 yds of yarn wool
              width   6″

Sett 28 ends per 1″

Total number of ends: 28 x 6 =   168
Selvedge double outside two   4
                                        172

Colour order – 1 black 1 white

Best warped in alternate strong colours, say black and white.

I is the correct way of showing this weave on point paper but
II is more convenient to weave. The result is the same in cloth.

Once the principle of a black top cloth and white bottom cloth is
understood there are no end of fascinating variations.

A. Reverse up and bottom cloths in varied widths
B. 'Fringe' one cloth left unwoven in strips
C. Padded pockets for upholstery
D. Tucks: Weave one inch on top cloth; release tension; weave
    two picks plain weave and beat up hard; restore tension. This
    is easier with two warp rollers.

It is recommended to set up a warp with alternate black and white threads. Using 11s cut wool, one would expect to have twice the number of threads per inch normally used for single cloth, i.e. 20 x 2, but it has been found easier to weave on a table loom at 30 or 36 ends per inch.

It is possible to weave Double Cloth by using the shuttle first to throw across the top cloth, then from right to left and back to the right side then to left – that is one pick on the top cloth, two on the lower cloth, then one on the top cloth. Supposing your original width of cloths was to be 20 inches, the result opens up to 40 inches. However, I do not recommend this as an experienced eye can always detect a line where the fold was. It is necessary not to have a selvedge threading at the fold line.

It is more satisfactory to weave a circular cloth, using the same shuttle weaving first top cloth, then returning for the lower cloth. This produces a tubular structure. It is usual to have the warp for both cloths in the same colour for both these two weaves.

By reversing the order of weaving, the top cloth can be placed below the back cloth for a few picks, then raised again, thus making a pattern of weft stripes. These can be varied in width. They can be padded with a thick thread, then a few picks woven in plain weave. Black warp threads can lie unwoven over the white cloth and even be cut as fringe and the process reversed. A few picks of plain weave to bind the two cloths better is needed if the fringe is to be cut.

Both warps can be striped, possibly at different intervals, producing many different decorations. If both warps are the same colour, it is possible to weave pockets by weaving tabby so far, then reverting to weave top cloth, returning to where the weave tabby stopped, then weaving the back cloth, continuing until a pocket is formed, then closing it with tabby and finishing the shed. Of course pockets can be left open at the top and filled with tiny toys for children by loving grandmothers.

With more shafts, multilayered cloth can be made, but these become complicated to weave without the aid of dobby mechanism.

In planning an overshot pattern to be woven on a four-shaft loom, it is necessary to arrange the draft so that the threads alternate between odd and even shafts to enable plain weave to be woven by lifting one and three then two and four shafts. The pattern can be divided between the four shafts, care being taken that the floats will never be too long. It is usual to weave the pattern by lifting shafts in pairs 12, 23, 34, 41, using a thicker thread than the yarn chosen for the ground weave. As there is a tabby pick between each pattern throw, the same pattern shaft can be lifted many times, making a block. It is by using the four different lifts in various order that the overshot is created.

An enterprising student, a teacher who came to my evening class for several years, had an ambition to weave a silk stole with a brocaded pattern. She looked at the American books and chose a draft christened Blooming Flower. Her plan was to weave a simple stripe border of about 18 inches a yard woven in full pattern. It was suggested that she inlaid the flower on a plain ground. In overshot weaves, every other line is plain weave. As long as a tabby pick is put every alternate pick between the pattern ones, cloth results. Each pattern pick can be repeated many times to make the figures. With a little thought, for the body of the stole she managed to inlay just the Flower, discarding the rest of the pattern. So that the cloth was not distorted, the Flowers inlaid were arranged in a five-end irregular satin formation across the cloth. We had chosen a 10/2s silk for the ground warp and used the same silk dyed a soft blue fourfold for the Flowers. Once the first flower was woven and the necessary boundaries of the draft identified, the stole grew swiftly.

Threading up an overshot pattern is a test of accuracy. Many have a long repeat and this must be checked and rechecked before continuing to thread the next repeat. It was prudent in my workshops to include only short examples, like Rosepath and Honeysuckle, as mini-examples.

Overshots

In all my 24 years of teaching design for woven textiles (1947–70), the overshot patterns were out of favour. To begin with, this was easy to understand; in 1947 materials were in short supply – clothing was on coupons – so everyone wanted to make tweed for sports jackets and suits. In two-hour weaving classes, if one had allowed a pupil to set up a coverlet, early American style, on one of our few treadle looms, it would be used by that person only for a year. By the 1950s, when we had plenty of looms, my students were busy winning Royal Society of Arts bursaries with contemporary dress or furnishing materials. Overshots were not in fashion.

An overshot pattern consists of a series of floats on a plain weave ground. The floats are in the weft and a thicker thread is chosen for this weft than that used for the ground weft, which is often the same count as the warp. Both warp and ground weft can be striped to enhance the design.

I have not included a draft for an overshot weave here as they did not fit well with my type of workshop. There are books specializing in these weaves. I would recommend every Guild weaver to try one. It is fascinating to see what elaborate pattern can be woven on a simple four shaft loom. But beware: each group of ends MUST be meticulously checked when threading the needles to avoid disaster.

In 1944, when stationed at Cardiff, I went one evening per week to a weaving class at the Art school for old times sake. I doubt whether I had even seen a loom since 1930 when I left the Textile Department at Leeds University. The teacher gave me a long overshot draft to thread. When woven it was unrecognisable!!! After analysis, it was discovered that I had solemnly included the selvedge in each repeat. Was my face red!!!